Same Training, Half the Time

Same Training, Half the Time

Delivering Results for Busy Learners

Kimberly Devlin

Trainers Publishing House
Johns Island, SC

TPH
www.trainerspublishinghouse.com
Email: info@trainerspublishinghouse.com

Ordering Information

Quantity Sales: sales@trainerspublishinghouse.com
Individual Sales: Amazon.com and Kindle.com

ISBN: 978-1-93924-709-4 (print)
ISBN: 978-1-93924-710-0 (ebook)

TPH
Publisher: Cat Russo
Editorial Director: Jacqueline Edlund-Braun
Rights Associate and Data Manager: Nancy Silva
Marketing: Dawn Baron, Passion Profits Consulting
Cover Design: Patty Sloniger Design, Houston, TX
Interior Design and Composition: PerfecType, Nashville, TN
Cover art: Fotolia

CONTENTS

INTRODUCTION

Same Training, Half the Time

- "Our management team wants the training time cut in half—now."
- "My stakeholders want to shorten the class length, but expect the same content to be covered."
- "The C-level team went to a conference. When they came back they told me I could only create micro-learning . . . and I'm not even sure what that is."
- "We aren't allowed to create any learning longer than *X* hours." (*X* often equals one or two.)
- "After I put my slides and speaker notes together, I was asked to cut my talk in *half*."

The details vary, but if you participate in the learning function in your organization, chances are good that you have said some version of these statements. They all come down to less time for training. But what hasn't been curtailed are the expectations of what training must accomplish. That leaves you and your fellow learning professionals wishing for a magic wand to wave that will produce the unicorn requested: "same training in half the time."

How Did We Get Here—Under This Time Crunch?

Multiple challenges are driving increased demands on learning:

1. **Listening Versus Learning.** What technology can accomplish in regard to *content transmission* is unquestionably impressive. Today's enhanced *speed of information* and *speed of communication* leave many people believing training should happen as quickly. And the pace shows no prospects of slowing. Content transmission is *not the same thing* as learning though. Read that last sentence again—it is foundational to the challenge of this book.
2. **Sausage Making.** To leaders and managers—even among the greatest learning champions—training is too often like sausage; they enjoy eating it but don't want to know how it is made. Without understanding the process for building a valued learning event and unaware of the repercussions of "pre-existing decisions" made without your input, many project sponsors make misguided requests.
3. **The Curse of High-Quality Courses.** When a program is designed exceptionally well, it appears simple. Simple and elegant, though, can be complex to create. Some instructional designers' work is so effective, so clear and direct, that it is hard for others to recognize all that went into creating it—as well as all that had to be left out of it. And this skews expectations.
4. **Lazy Learners.** Just as watching a weight-loss-challenge reality TV show from one's couch does nothing for one's waistline, passively listening to a person who possesses a skill does little to transfer that skill. Learning is not a passive activity. It takes effort, and when the framework for that effort isn't built into the course design, lazy learners are created. Because lazy learners don't learn, managers see training time as wasted time. And that results in them affording less time for future learning events.
5. **Paid-Vacation Model of Training.** We pay a high price for bad training and short-sighted design plans. When time, effort, and money are spent to develop employees' skills, and they perform after training as they did before it, managers are right to consider training time as paid vacation. Even when skills

are acquired and employees initially shift their behaviors post-training, if no one is acknowledging, tracking, measuring, or reinforcing the behavior changes because of short-sighted designs, the employees will slip back to old patterns. The result, again, is that learning is ineffective. This reinforces managers' perceptions that training time = wasted time. So, again, they afford less time for training.

I am certain you can list additional reasons from your own experience. I invite you to share them on my blog. Check out KimberlyDevlin.com.

Magic Wands and Fairy Dust—On Backorder Indefinitely

Can 10 pounds of training fit into a 5-pound bag? That is the conundrum of requests for the same training in half the time. And there isn't a quick-fix answer that fits into a Tweet. Truthfully, training condensed into less time can easily require more time to create. Mark Twain is credited with writing "I'd have written you a shorter letter, but I didn't have the time." Whether he wrote it or not, it applies to your challenge of packing training into ever-smaller packages.

Currently, in an effort to meet this goal, you and your training team may be:

- Shifting the burden to learners with a "pre-work dump."
- Cutting out application activities.
- Forgoing adequate scaffolding for and debriefing of exercises.
- Ending sessions with "we can cover the rest next time."
- Spending nights and weekends attempting to create inappropriate deliverables and meet unrealistic deadlines for programs that don't add value.

And, to what end? To overhear lunchroom conversations describing training as painful? To watch the measure of your success stop with a checkmark beside "training done"? To read evaluations in which learners describe sessions as exhausting data dumps?

Something Has to Give

You can't have the *same* training in half the time. You can't. But you can have *better* training in half the time. In fact, here is the good news of this book:

- You can develop shorter trainings that deliver meaningful results.
- You can condense existing programs into shorter events that the business values.
- You can satisfy learners' desire for effective, on-demand learning experiences that respect their time and attention spans.
- You can achieve better results with shorter events than you currently do with longer programs.
- And—the best news of all—instead of continuing to fulfill potentially misguided training requests at a breakneck pace, with the strategies in this book, you can shift from reacting to training requests you receive to driving what training looks like in your organization!

Getting to better training in half the time will certainly include design choices, and you will find Chapters 5, 6, and 7 full of them. But better training can easily require additional upfront time to develop the solution and will unquestionably require selective choices regarding content. So, earlier chapters will help you strategize how to gain more time, tighter scopes, an improved list of deliverables, and other key approaches, as well as provide a method to distill vast quantities of program content down to the essentials. Ready?

How Can This Book Help You Create and Deliver Meaningful Learning Events With Less Stress?

Do you want a reputation for building highly desired, sought-after programs? Would you like to develop your skills for creating programs that actually help employees perform better? Do you want business partners to say that your learning events are practical, mission-critical, and value-added? And would you like to achieve those things while managing a work/life balance and enjoying the work you do?

Start by identifying your role in training. Choose the option that most closely describes how you participate in the training function in your organization:

- ❑ I am an instructional designer and live these frustrations on a daily basis.
- ❑ I am a human resources (HR) professional caught between misguided requests from the business and our internal and external training partners working to fulfill them.
- ❑ I am a member of the management team and, yes, I do make requests to "cover it all in less time"—we just don't have the luxury of long learning events and we need employees to be service ready out of the gate.
- ❑ I am a professional, sometimes known as a subject matter expert (SME), who has been tasked with training others, but I have no background in adult learning—I sometimes feel I am in over my head.
- ❑ I am a trainer and see participants struggle to process the volume of information being thrown at them in learning events as I struggle to cover it all.

Next, with your answer in mind, consider which navigational approach to this book will serve you best.

Option 1: Start at the Beginning

Reading and working through the chapters in sequential order (yes, there will be exercises for you to complete) may be best if:

- You are an instructional designer.
- You are an HR professional.

The consultative skills of the early chapters will help you gain—or regain—control of your work or the projects you oversee. And the newfound influence on projects' direction and respect from your business partners you will gain by applying the techniques there will enhance your effectiveness in implementing later chapters' design choice ideas. The result? The innovative design recommendations you propose will meet with less resistance; be more fun to integrate and develop; and generate better outcomes for you, your partners, and the learners in your courses.

Option 2: Jump Around

With the second option, let the roadmap in the box (Figure I-1) guide how you navigate the chapters, worksheets, and resources if:

- You are in need of a quick fix for a specific project challenge, regardless of your role.
- You are a trainer, and your content-heavy deliveries are in need of an infusion of interactivity.
- You are a manager, SME, or HR professional who is on the margins of a design project and are looking for examples and inspiration to help inform how you contribute to the project in a meaningful way.
- You need a grounding in, or a touchstone moment with, the foundations of adult learning and the science of the instructional design process—regardless of your role—before getting into specific strategies.

The structure of the book assumes the majority of readers are instructional designers. The tone speaks directly to them. If you are one, great. If you are not, hold on before you move on—read the book as a conversation—as if sitting in a consultation between the instructional designer and me. You will find strategies and guidance for your projects, and you will be able to glean from the discussion ways that you can contribute to the learning process more effectively.

You will also want to complete the assessment and start your action planning using the tools in Chapter 10.

You Can Do It—This Book Can Help

No matter your role or level of expertise in helping people learn and perform better in their jobs, you are in the role for a reason. It may be your educational credentials, skills you demonstrate in a different function, a natural talent recognized by another, or something else. And, up until now, you have

FIGURE I-1. ROADMAP TO FINDING WHAT YOU NEED

- **Table of Contents:** Gain insight on what each chapter can do for you, and the questions that frame each chapter may direct you to an in-the-moment challenge you need to resolve.
- **Chapters 1–3:** Get ahead of challenging training requests with these chapters that focus on managing expectations by developing your consultative skills for project management and project design.
- **Chapter 4:** Learn a simple—but not simplistic—process for isolating the essential content from all the potentially valuable content that could be considered for inclusion in a course.
- **Chapters 5–7:** Leverage your design choices: specifically, how to extend where a learning event begins and ends, position learners for success before they arrive, design for successes during the event, and sustain the momentum of those successes after the event. These chapters will help you to achieve the goal of all workplace learning—behavior change—and turn your time-squeezed learning events into highly desired, results-driven learning experiences.
- **Chapter 8:** Part One will serve as a touchstone for experienced learning and development (L&D) professionals and will provide a succinct grounding in instructional design theory and process for managers, SMEs, or trainers with limited instructional design experience. Part Two is dedicated to looking at this topic through the non-instructional designer lens. For example, how can you, as a manager who is collaborating with a designer, best support him and remove roadblocks that impede getting to the desired outcome? As a trainer, what are you to do when you're told training time will be cut, but there is no instructional designer involved to tighten the course length and decide what to keep and leave out? Begin here if you have limited instructional design experience.
- **Chapter 9:** Receive a reminder that better training in half the time is within your reach—in fact, it is within your control!
- **Chapter 10:** Get the tools. This chapter is a repository of worksheets, assessments, and job aids that will help you create better training in half the time.

likely been working hard to meet expectations. Now you can start working smarter and *exceed expectations*. And you can even have more fun.

The time crunch has always been an instructional design problem to be solved, but it is also a fantastic opportunity to innovate, explore creative alternatives, and find new ways to achieve improved results. There is no one right way to achieve better training in half the time, but one thing is for sure: Bad training hurts everyone. Use the strategies, ideas, and resources of this book to cultivate a seat at the decision-making table of your organization, develop new partnerships and better relationships with your learning sponsors, and deliver effective training that is enjoyed by learners. *Same Training, Half the Time* will up your game whether you face a time crunch or not.

1

How Do I Achieve the Impossible?

A 5-Step Communication Strategy to Move the Finish Line

Having established (and accepted) that you can't accomplish it all in half the time, the first step to delivering *better* training in half the time is managing expectations, and that will require a persuasive communication strategy. I have developed a communication strategy—the Five A's: Appreciate, Acknowledge, Ask, Apprehension, and Alternatives—that will help you adjust project expectations and also:

- Build rapport with project partners.
- Gather critical needs analysis information.
- Enhance the value placed on your expertise and skills.
- Provide learners with better experiences.
- Achieve greater organizational results from the learning solutions ultimately developed.

Let's back up a moment. If you are fortunate, you have clients, stakeholders, and executive team members who have a true appreciation for what goes into creating quality learning events. They may not be able to explain the complete process, but they know there is one. And they trust you and your expertise to follow it. If you fall into that category, set this book aside for a moment and call each of those people to thank them. They make your work easier and more fulfilling. They also enable you to invest your time in the actions that translate into real results as an outcome of employees participating in training. (I am not kidding. Really, go call them!) The Five A's will easily integrate into your project request meetings with these collaborative-minded individuals.

If you, however, are not so fortunate, grab a highlighter—you'll want it as you continue! Know that you are in good company. More often than not, an instructional designer's first task in creating a learning event is conducting an "embedded learning event"—educating the customer. Using the Five A's in your project request discussions will create teaching moments, provide the framework to guide clients to better outcomes, and, when used consistently, transition you into a work environment where your knowledge and abilities are recognized and valued—an enviable place to be.

Whichever camp you fall into, when you receive a request for the "same training in half the time," you will want to move the finish line before beginning to run the race. Moving the finish line means adjusting expectations. That may translate to reining in the deliverables. It may mean distributing the workload in new or creative ways. Perhaps it will mean finding middle ground regarding the duration of training, or allocating more time for you to build the training. It may even mean developing an entirely different vision of the end result (for example, instead of a shorter instructor-led training—ILT—course, the final product may be a series of leader-led activities that are embedded in existing staff meetings). Adjusting the expectations can be minor or major—and in either case it will be critical. For a few additional examples of what moving the finish line might look like, check out Figure 1-1.

> **Insider Tip**
>
> **Focus on the Donut—Not the Hole**
>
> Small shifts count. Focus less on how far the line gets moved and more on moving it. This will build momentum for bigger shifts on future projects.

Before you say that isn't an option for you because training requests are nonnegotiable where you work (Too late? Have you said it already?), let me suggest that *everything* is negotiable. You just have to be willing to walk away. Let's soften that—you have to be willing to walk away or be invested in the long-term win, like the coach who is more focused on winning the season than on winning a given game. You might not come out of the negotiation with additional course time or fewer content demands on your *current* project (that is, this *game* may count in the loss column), but if you negotiate from a broader perspective and integrate agreements for *subsequent* training requests, you likely will gain time or reduce scope on *all* future projects (that is, win the season and take home the trophy!)

FIGURE 1-1. MOVING THE FINISH LINE

Move the finish line . . .		
. . . An inch or a foot	**. . . 50 yards**	**. . . a mile**
• Take a phased approach to the project. Deliverables may not change, but the implementation schedule can. • Shift the training delivery channel to one more conducive to learners' needs than the one requested or envisioned. • Enlist support and resources from the project requestor's team to ease the time crunch on you or your team.	• Divide your e-learning course components into three categories and allow learners to select their participation level: – core (required) – critical (highly recommended) – complementary (optional)	• Convert a request for a short instructor-led training to a series of leader-led activities embedded into existing staff meetings. • Play the devil's advocate and ask: "If we didn't have this training, what would be the cost?" to start a conversation to explore alternative solutions—such as shorter training or perhaps no training at all.

Managing Expectations With the Five A's

Moving the finish line requires persuasive communication. In the battle between your opinion (the learning professional) and their opinion (the program sponsors), the sponsors' opinion will usually win out. So, you need to choose a better strategy than mere opinions—which you can do by integrating the Five A's: Appreciate, Acknowledge, Ask, Apprehension, Alternatives.

To connect the Five A's model to your reality, select the situation that most closely resembles your current challenge—or write your own—and keep it in mind as you work through the steps that follow:

1. A business unit wants a half-day program developed—and presented you with enough learning goals to justify multiple half-day sessions.
2. Metrics indicate learners are abandoning a 45-minute, self-paced e-learning class less than half-way through; the director wants it cut to no more than 20 minutes.
3. You received a request to deliver a customized version of an existing three-day course. The requesting agency envisions five or six "hard-hitting" one-hour sessions that "leave out the fluffy stuff."
4. You are scheduled to facilitate a program for a new client. After reviewing the learning objectives and topics, they ask you to eliminate certain sections, but the sections they want to delete are foundational to achieving the goal they have in mind.
5. A senior manager in the department that does the most hiring tells you that the full-day NEO—new employee orientation—needs to be distilled to a half-day format but still cover all of the existing content because she needs the new hires operation-ready when they get to the warehouse floor after lunch. She shares that it shouldn't be too hard if you cut out all the socializing components that are wasted time and just tell them what they need to know.
6. Something else you are contending with: ________________________

   ____

(Note: Chapter 10 includes an assessment, worksheet, and job aid that will support you in using the Five A's. For now, knowing and keeping your situation in mind will be sufficient as you are introduced to the Five A's model.)

So, with your situation clearly in mind, here is the 10,000-feet view of the model:

Step 1: Appreciate—Convey genuine thanks for being brought in on the potential project and enhance your understanding of the request.

Step 2: Acknowledge—Recognize the criticality of the request.

Step 3: Ask—Clarify details of the request while creating space for the possibility that—as presented—it may not be the best solution.

Step 4: Apprehension—Raise key concerns in a nonconfrontational manner.

Step 5: Alternatives—Present options that factor in what you have learned in the prior steps and that are informed by your experience and expertise.

Implementing this communication model will not be a monologue—it will be a dialogue framed by these five sequential elements. The ground-level view of the model in the rest of this chapter explains each element and provides language to use and tips to follow. Review the Insider Tip on the next page for advice on making the Five A's work for you as you integrate the technique into your day-to-day practices. At the end of the chapter, there are worked examples of the five sample scenarios—but please don't jump ahead to them. Refer to the worked examples after your ground-level tour.

Step 1: Appreciate

Training is expendable. That may be a difficult concept to accept, but it is true. Internal training teams are commonly a cost center, external consultants are an expense, learning events create opportunity costs by taking employees away from performing their jobs, and many courses and classes create no measurable improvement in performance. You can likely add your own reasons why training has been classified as expendable from your experience.

Insider Tip

How to Make the Five A's Work for You

The Five A's can be a powerful tool to manage expectations with your stakeholders. For best success, keep these tips in mind:

Personalize:

- **Adapt the scripts.** Make them fit your personality while maintaining the intent of each step.
- **Write your own versions of the sample language.** Do this now, as you are reading.
- **Modify selected language.** Tailor it to your project, sponsor, and organizational culture.

Prepare:

- **Go in informed.** Research the project, the department, and the players.
- **Draft your plan.** Write down planned phrases based on your pre-meeting research. Keep in mind the saying: failing to plan equals planning to fail.
- **Expect to revise your plan.** Anticipate multiple ways to connect your plan, in sequential order, with the information you receive in the discussion.
- **Bring your plan and refer to it as needed.**

Practice:

- **Know your opener.** Be ready to start with your prepared Appreciate phrase (see Step 1).
- **Develop your comfort level.** Some behind-the-scenes practice with a colleague is highly recommended so that your communication sounds natural, organic, and effortless, especially if this kind of questioning and communication approach is new to you.

For all these reasons, every time you receive a request to provide a learning solution, be thankful and express your gratitude. It is helpful to keep in mind that the training sponsors had a choice, and they chose to consider training as vital.

To show your appreciation for being asked to help, consider which of the following statements are appropriate to your situation. Then write a few of your own that follow the spirit of these to have ready when needed:

- "Thank you for letting me talk through this with you."
- "I appreciate your thinking about performance support in relation to this initiative."
- "It is always a pleasure to explore needs with your team."
- "Thank you for thinking of me to look at this with you."
- "I am grateful for the advance notice on this project request—this doesn't always happen."
- "Thank you for your call."
- ____________________
- ____________________
- ____________________

Insider Tip

Sincerity and genuine appreciation are essential. And it isn't enough to just say the words; you need to mean them.

If you read those with a keen eye, you noticed they are expressing appreciation for being *called in*. They intentionally, and strategically, leave a lot of latitude regarding what the final outcome will be. If you don't see that immediately, try comparing the phrases above to these that follow, which are *not* recommended:

✘ "Thank you for asking me to shorten this course for you."
✘ "I appreciate that you see training is needed to support this initiative."
✘ "Thank you for thinking of me to create this training."
✘ "My sincere thanks for the advance notice on your course development need."

The challenge of the second set of phrases is that you are committing to a specific outcome—a shortened class or creating training—right from the start of the conversation. And that might not be what is in the best interests of the requestor or the eventual learners.

After comparing the two sets of Appreciate phrases, above, reread those you wrote. Will any of them benefit from a bit of editing? Recast them here if needed:

- ____
- ____
- ____

The Appreciate step is about two forms of appreciation—gratitude and understanding. Having expressed a genuine statement of gratitude (addressed above) you will want to learn as much as you can about what the requestor envisions to develop your understanding of her mindset. Doing so will position you to inject Acknowledge, the next A, into the discussion. You can gather information to develop your awareness with broad questions such as:

- "What can you tell me about why you want to do this now?"
- "What or who is the driving force behind this request?"
- "How did you arrive at this proposed course of action?"
- "Were there alternative approaches you considered or tried?"

Listen. Take notes. Make eye-contact. Nod your head in recognition of key points made. And, ask clarifying questions as needed.

With a solid grasp of the thought processes and events that led to the request, you are ready to integrate Acknowledge into the discussion and then transition to Ask.

Step 2: Acknowledge

The second element, Acknowledge, is all about recognizing the importance of the project sponsor's request—and doing so in a way that maintains neutrality on the ultimate direction the request will take.

A friend of mine practices Aikido, one of the martial arts. From him, I have learned that blocking a punch requires meeting it with equal force—the more energy in the punch, the more energy required to stop it. And equal force only stops the punch between you. To reverse the direction of the punch requires exerting even more force than it initially carried. I am probably oversimplifying this, but as I understand it, there are two options for an Aikido defender. First, exert energy—meet the punch with equal force (to stop it) or with greater force (to redirect it). Or, second, blend with the energy—get out of the way, let the opponent go forward, and then use their momentum and your energy to more easily and effectively redirect the punch. The philosophy of Aikido is in the meaning of each character: *ai* = harmonize, *ki* = energy, and *do* = the way.

Insider Tip

Appreciate and Acknowledge are relationship builders. The respect you demonstrate in these steps will help build rapport with project partners.

We can apply the Aikido philosophy to Acknowledge if we think of validating the requestor's ideas as harmonizing with them. By acknowledging the request, we are blending with its energy and its forward momentum rather than trying to block it with force and redirect it—say, by detailing a list of reasons why the request is wrong, doesn't meet the true need, or won't be effective. My grandmother used to say this another way: "You attract more bees with honey than vinegar." Please be patient at this point in the process: The redirect will come at Step 5, Alternatives.

So, the goal of Acknowledge is to be supportive of the request (and the requestor) without committing to delivering on what has been requested in the exact form it has been requested; you are preparing to transition to the exploratory phase of the conversation.

Consider the following starters to build upon or craft your own Acknowledgement statement that aligns with the information you know about the request:

- "I understand how critical this is."
- "I can see where you are coming from."
- "Certainly, it makes sense that the staff/team/group will need support in the transition."

- "Yes, I agree that time is precious, and I recognize the operational constraints your team works within."
- "I can see you have given this a great deal of thought."
- "I do see the path of events that brought you to this point."
- "Yes, I can certainly appreciate the position you are in."
- "This all makes sense as you have laid it out."

Unlike Aikido, your project relationship—hopefully—will not be a battle. Preferably it will be a collaboration, a partnership, or at least a cordial working relationship. Certainly, some stakeholders who make misguided or challenging requests are demanding. More often than not, though, they are merely uninformed about the process required for an adult to learn a skill, master it, and transfer it to on-the-job performance. Equally true, there is a strong possibility your stakeholder has a problem to fix and sees you as being able to provide a solution to it. For these reasons, being empathetic to their situation and demonstrating that empathy in the discussion become significant. For example, the person who contacted you with the request may be answering to a senior staff member, be stressed over meeting a directive, or see you and training as their last hope to correct an ongoing problem. Sincere empathy will build a foundation for a collaborative approach to the project and increase your successes with the subsequent steps of the model.

Step 3: Ask

After sharing sincere gratitude and genuinely acknowledging the criticality of the request, step three—Ask—uses questioning and paraphrasing to clarify the request while opening the way for a client to envision the possibility of something other than exactly what she requested. It isn't about strong-arming her into agreeing that you know better than she does. It is about using your strategically crafted questions to hold a mirror up to her request that allows her to see whether she truly wants what she is asking for, or to become receptive to alternatives you can propose.

Here is the key question stem I use:

- "Am I hearing you correctly that. . . . ?"

Don't be lulled into thinking this is an easy question stem to complete. Remember that Ask is about using *strategically crafted questions* to prepare the conversation to easily veer toward any of a multitude of directions.

A potential mistake in completing the Ask sentence stem "Am I hearing you correctly that . . ." is restating back the packaged set of expectations the client shared with you. For example, in the context of sample scenario 5—NEO training for warehouse new hires—avoid saying "If I have this right, you want the current 8-hour new hire orientation to be delivered in a half-day format, ensuring all of the current material is addressed, and resulting in new hires being fully onboarded. Is that correct?"

Instead, break down the stated desired outcome into its individual building blocks. This will create greater flexibility in how the pieces may, or may not, fit into the final solution. Use a conversational approach instead of a rapid-fire succession of statements. Here's an example:

"Am I correct that your priority is reducing the length of the current new hire orientation?" (Notice "half-day" as a specific timing goal has been left out.)

Wait for a reply.

If the answer is no, determine what the top priority is.

If the answer is yes, you might ask "What makes 4 hours the ideal timeframe?"

Based on the reply, you may be able to follow up with "So, we may have some flexibility there?"

Consider the sample conversation flow in Figure 1-2.

FIGURE 1-2. SAMPLE ASK CONVERSATION FLOW CHART

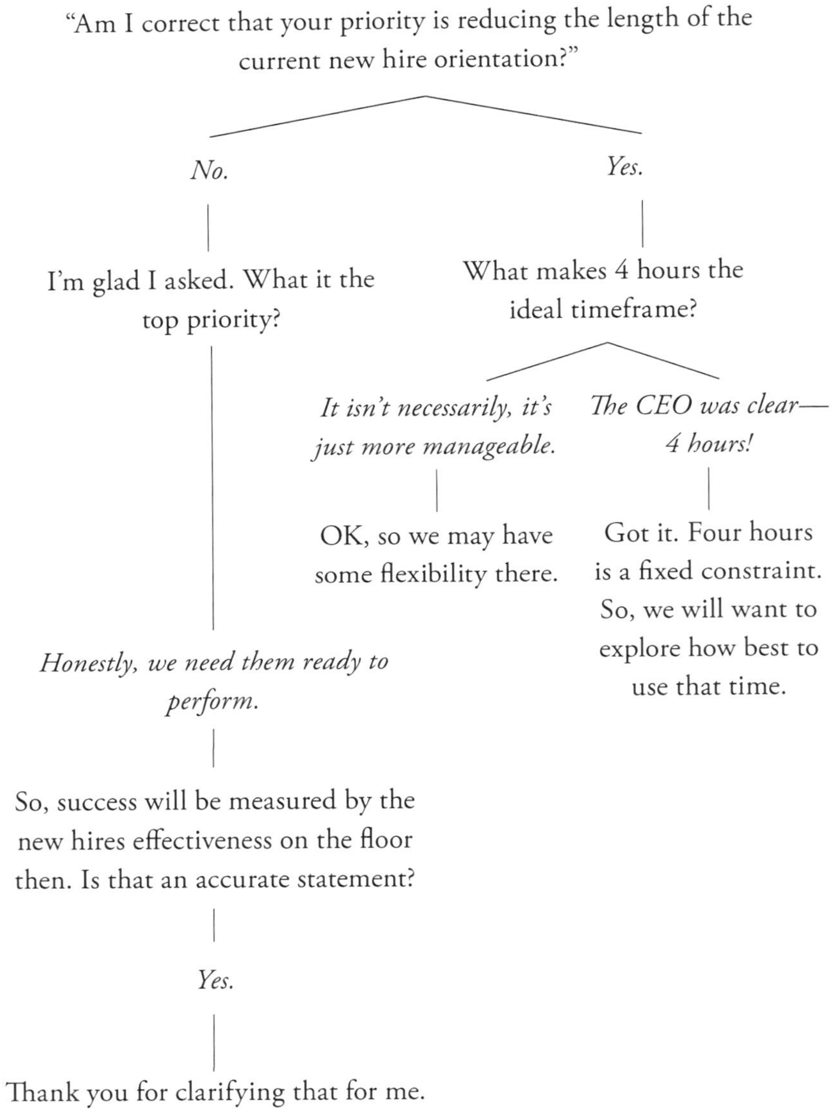

"Am I correct that your priority is reducing the length of the current new hire orientation?"

No.

I'm glad I asked. What it the top priority?

Honestly, we need them ready to perform.

So, success will be measured by the new hires effectiveness on the floor then. Is that an accurate statement?

Yes.

Thank you for clarifying that for me.

Yes.

What makes 4 hours the ideal timeframe?

It isn't necessarily, it's just more manageable.

OK, so we may have some flexibility there.

The CEO was clear—4 hours!

Got it. Four hours is a fixed constraint. So, we will want to explore how best to use that time.

From here, move to the next building block of the initially stated desired outcome—"ensuring all the current material is addressed." Staying with this example, a few of these questions may be appropriate:

- "Can you tell me more about your thoughts on keeping all of the content?"
- "Have you had a chance to speak with recent new hires, to confirm how they are using all the material in the current program?"
- "Where did the current body of content come from? Can you share the history of the course design with me?"
- "Do you know when the existing course was developed . . . I'm asking so that I can get a sense if any of the content may be dated—as in outdated?"

After some exploration of the current contents, address the "genie in the bottle" portion of the request—"new hires being fully onboarded"—with additional questions:

- "What do you mean, exactly, when you say *fully onboarded*?"
- "What essential skills and knowledge need to be mastered in this session?"
- "How will we define *mastery* for this program?"

Take a few minutes now to think through your situation. Compare it to the NEO example above. What sample language from the scenario can you use or tailor to your needs? What additional language will you craft? Remember that you are using Ask to paraphrase elements of the original request while listening for areas of flexibility and fixed constraints. This information will allow you to craft your Alternatives (Step 5) for greatest receptivity.

Step 3, Ask, is typically the lengthiest portion of the conversation. You want to explore each of the building blocks in the initial request here. Start each portion of this step with open-ended questions. Follow up with probing questions to clarify answers and be prepared with questions that align with any path your conversation's flow may follow.

Step 4: Apprehension

When transitioning from Ask to Apprehension, use this effective opening:

- "Here is my one concern. . . ."

If this sentence stem feels confrontational to you, Figure 1-3 gives several ways you can soften it. Each example that follows has a different priority concern—there may be any number of priority concerns based on the conversation up until this point.

FIGURE 1-3. STEP 4 APPREHENSION PHRASES

Start with: →	*"Here is my one concern. . . ."*
Follow with: →	*". . . and let me tell you upfront, we can overcome it."*
Then state your priority concern: →	*"I'm just concerned that if we cut the time so drastically, without prioritizing what to include and what to pare down, the learners will be drinking from a fire hose and take nothing away other than feeling overwhelmed. I remember my first day here–there was a lot to take in."*

Start with: →	*"Here is my one concern. . . ."*
Follow with: →	*". . . and it is less of a concern and more of an observation really."*
Then state your priority concern: →	*"I'm just processing all that you have shared, and if the measure of success that you will be held to is new hires' effectiveness on the floor, it seems that it is in everyone's best interests to make that the focus of our plan instead of the course length as the priority. And I already have a number of ideas in support of that which I would like to share with you."*

Start with: →	*"Here is my one concern. . . ."*
Follow with: →	*". . . and I am raising it now to be realistic."*
Then state your priority concern: →	*"As I am listening to you, I am making notes on the deliverables required to make this a successful initiative for you. And, believe me, I am thrilled you see the value of them. Here is the thing: In addition to the course itself, we need to build evaluation instruments, job aids, management support tools, a communication plan and its messaging, and a train-the-trainer. And those are just what we have identified so far. My real concern here is the timeline. To do all this and do it right, we really should reconsider the proposed deadline."*

Start with: →	*"Here is my one concern. . . ."*
Follow with: →	*". . . which I am confident we can resolve."*
Then state your priority concern: →	*"It dawns on me that the current content and design of the 8-hour program isn't getting you the results you need. So, I am not seeing how condensing the same material into less time for the new hires to master is going to achieve what you want. That said, one of my strengths is developing learning objectives that directly support the needs of the business—and that will guide us in refining which content the new hires really need. We may even find we need new content in place of some of what we already have."*

If "here is my one concern" still feels too strong, consider these alternatives:

- "We certainly could do that. I'm just thinking about ________ and contemplating how we can best avoid ________."
- "We certainly could do that. I'm just worried you're not going to get the results you're looking for."

When you are entering this stage of the conversation, you may actually have more than one concern. Determine which is your greatest concern and begin with it. If there are other issues, listen for opportunities to weave them into the discussion using transitions such as:

- "You raise a good point, we really should be considering/thinking about *X* as well."
- "Now that you say that, I do have another question for you. . . ."
- "Have you or your team already *X*'d, or will we need to consider options there?"
- "How can the training team support you in addressing the issue of . . . ?"

Again, take notes on the discussion at this stage. You will want to integrate the comments and ideas that the requestor shares into the last step, Alternatives.

Try This

"I keep hearing you say that the constraint on training time is based on your limited budget. Can you connect the dots on that for me—is it tied to development costs? Anticipated materials costs? Reserving off-site training space? Something else? The better I understand the constraint, the more creative I can get in working within or around it."

Step 5: Alternatives

After building a foundation of respect and trust in the initial steps of Appreciate and Acknowledge, and creating space for flexibility in the project approach during Ask and Apprehension, the final step, Alternatives, is where the finish line can be moved to a more realistic—but more important, beneficial—goal.

You likely came into the project scoping conversation with ideas on the best direction to take, based on preliminary information shared with you in the initial request and your own preparatory research. Ideally, during the meeting you have been modifying and tailoring those ideas based on the information learned in the discussion. Now it is time to present your alternatives—or, on a complex request, propose that you will develop suggested approaches to present in the coming days.

Now

Let's assume that you will go with the first option of presenting alternatives on the spot. When proposing alternatives, be sure to frame them so that you:

> **Insider Tip**
> It is okay to reconvene with your alternatives. Reconvening can do a few things for you. It affords time to think through the options you will propose, bounce ideas off of peers, and establish a solid vision of what the deliverables, time commitments, costs, roles, responsibilities, and so on will be.

- ✓ Keep elements of the original request in your suggested alternatives.
- ✓ Draw parallels to your prior successful projects and experience.
- ✓ Clearly state how your alternatives will benefit the requestor.

Consider moving into Alternatives with "starter language" such as the following:

- "When you suggested that we __________, that sparked an idea for me. . . ."
- "I certainly hear where you're coming from. Are you open to hearing how I see this and some slightly different approaches?"
- "Initially, this may sound radically different than what you're asking for, but it has the same foundational elements, and I believe it will be a great way to get to your goal."
- "I get the feeling that you are receptive to additional ideas. What would you think of . . . ?"
- "I'd like to run a few ideas past you to see what your thoughts are on them."

As you present your alternatives, the following language can be used to connect your ideas to the project sponsor's ideas and to connect your ideas to the goal she is looking to achieve:

- "You suggested that we _________, and I agree that we should do that [or some specific part of it you agree with]. I would only add that we should also _________."
- "What would you say if I suggested that we think about _____."
- "Based on my experience on previous projects, I'm confident we'll have greater success in reaching your goal if we consider. . . ."
- "Based on prior projects' experiences, I'd like to suggest a few alternatives for your consideration."
- "Based on prior projects, I recommend _________."
- "I'm thinking out loud here, but here is what is coming to mind for me—and I'd really like your input on this. . . ."
- "So, what if we. . . ."
- "What if, instead of *X*, we were to _______________?"
- "Do you know what I think would really get you where you're looking to be on this project? I suggest we should think about _____________."

If you meet resistance, the following phrases can allow you to remain persistent without being perceived as pushy:

- "Ultimately, the final decision will be yours; I would just like to strongly suggest you consider. . . ."
- "I would like to suggest we stay open to the idea of _________."
- "If you are still open to alternative ideas—which I think will get you greater results—I'm happy to put together some thoughts to show to you."
- "I really want this project to be a success for you. Would it be okay for me to mock up some examples of what I am envisioning for your review? We can walk through the examples together and see what will work best."

Later

Let's now consider the second option—in which you adjourn and return with alternatives. If proposing alternatives on the spot isn't advisable, and it may not be for many reasons—time is tight, your thoughts are not fully formed, you want to review a few prior projects, you need to review existing commitments to determine timelines, and so on—here are some phrases you can use to transition to closing this conversation and create space to return with a proposal. A typical transition might sound like this:

> "Thank you for all that you have shared. I feel I now have a much stronger understanding of your goals and your constraints."
>
> "As I see it, we have some options. And options are always good."
>
> "I'd like to put together some approaches for you based on everything you have shared and some ideas I have bouncing around. Can I have *X* days to draft something up to show you?"

In this case, when you reconvene to review your Alternatives, be sure to infuse the second conversation with details learned in the first conversation. Appreciate and Acknowledge phrases will continue to build rapport. Connecting your recommendations back to the areas of flexibility you identified during Ask will go a long way toward providing the sponsor with idea ownership—which gains buy in. And be sure to explain how your ideas resolve the concerns raised in Apprehension. For example:

> "May I say once more that I am honored and excited to be working with you on this project [Appreciate]. As I was working on developing these ideas for you, I repeatedly turned to the outline you drafted for our first meeting. Thank you for creating it as it made my work easier [Acknowledge]. I am particularly excited about an idea I have to meet your goal of connecting the learning environment with learners' work environment [Ask]. Remember how you said *X* . . . well, that gave me an idea to . . . [Ask and Acknowledge]. The beauty of this idea—and I have you to thank for it—is that it eliminates the challenge we were worried about with ___________" [Acknowledge and Apprehension]. I identified a few apps that will allow us to [details of your proposed ideas] . . . [Alternatives]."

The Five A's Applied in Five Scenarios

Here are a few outlines of how the model could work in the sample situations presented earlier in the chapter. Now that you are familiar with the model, have read through sample phrases, and have crafted some language tailored to your situation, compare your implementation ideas with these. Keep in mind that the outlines only show your side of the conversation; you will want to ensure you have a dialogue with the project sponsor.

After working through this section, complete the Chapter 1 Assessment: Using the Five A's to Move the Finish Line included in Chapter 10. Also provided there are a worksheet for Using the Five A's to Move the Finish Line and a job aid of Language Aligned With the Five A's for Moving the Finish Line, which pulls into one place all of the sample phrases introduced throughout this chapter.

Scenario 1. A business unit wants a half-day program developed—and presented you with enough learning goals to justify multiple half-day sessions.

- **Appreciate**—Thank you for asking me to look at this with you.
- **Acknowledge**—It is obvious that you have already put a lot of thought into this. Thank you for providing me with your working list of draft learning goals.
- **Ask**—Out of everything on this list, which topics will be most critical? In other words, which will be foundational to the learners' success? Which will get them closest to where you want them to be?
- **Apprehension**—Here is what I am a bit concerned about. When I first looked over this list—and don't get me wrong, it is a great list and I can see why these items are on here—but when I look at it and you tell me it is all essential, I can easily see needing multiple sessions to address all of this content in a meaningful way. I know you want the learning to stick.
- **Alternatives**—So, I am wondering what latitude we have here. For example, would you be open to considering bringing the learners together for more than one session? Or, can we propose a solution that includes some self-paced learning activities to

address select content? And, is there select content that may be better provided as job aids? These are some of the thoughts coming to me. Because I hear you saying that all of the content is essential, and I know we all want to be sure we are setting up the learners for success. It is a tremendous amount to achieve in 3.5 hours. Thoughts?

Scenario 2. Metrics indicate learners are abandoning a 45-minute, self-paced e-learning class less than half-way through; the director wants it cut to no more than 20 minutes.

- **Appreciate**—Thank you for your call.
- **Acknowledge**—I'd also like to thank you for taking the time to study the metrics on this program. Too often training initiatives are undertaken to "check off a box" that training was provided. I can certainly understand your concern over course completion rates.
- **Ask**—Have you had time to dig deeper than the training report? For example, do we know why learners haven't been completing the course?
- **Apprehension**—Before we jump ahead to possible solutions for the current situation, I'd like to suggest we get some answers to these questions.
- **Alternatives**—As I see it, the reasons behind the numbers should be driving the solution. For example, let's walk through three possible causes other than "it is too long." If learners are expecting a shorter program and are not scheduling enough time to complete it, the answer may be as easy as indicating the estimated duration in the invitation email and onscreen prior to starting the program. Another possibility is that the design isn't interactive enough or targeted at the appropriate level of challenge, resulting in learners perceiving it as a waste of time even though they are interested in the topic. In that case, rework will obviously be needed, but the duration may not be the concern. Perhaps the harshest reason may be the topic simply isn't valued. In which case, I'd respectfully question if we should be redesigning it at all?

Scenario 3. You received a request to deliver a customized version of an existing three-day course. The requesting agency envisions five or six "hard-hitting" one-hour sessions that "leave out the fluffy stuff."

- **Appreciate**—I am thrilled to hear that you see value of our *X* course.
- **Acknowledge**—I also agree with you that the skills it focuses on align with your goals for this effort and that we can modify the delivery format effectively for you.
- **Ask**—Before we get too far into the planning, can you tell me what you mean by "fluffy stuff" and your thought process behind eliminating it?
- **Apprehension**—That is helpful, thank you. Here is the challenge I see in what you have proposed—the activities you are asking to skip are where the learning is happening. And while they *are* fun for the learners—by design—they are not actually games. I agree that we can tighten the time; I'd just ask you to place your trust in my experience when we get down to choosing what to keep, what to drop, and what to modify.
- **Alternatives**—In the proposed one-hour format, we will certainly need to make adjustments. I'd like to get your approval for me to draft a sample session or two that we can review together; this will give us concrete examples to work with and allow me to show you how hard-hitting interactive can be!

Scenario 4. You are scheduled to facilitate an existing program for a new client. After reviewing the learning objectives and topics, they ask you to eliminate certain sections, but the sections they want to delete are foundational to achieving the goal they have in mind.

- **Appreciate**—Thank you for scheduling this call with me before the delivery.
- **Acknowledge**—It is obvious that you are heavily vested in this being a success based on the time you have taken to review the agenda in such detail. Thank you for that.
- **Ask**—Can you tell me your thoughts behind selecting those sections for possible deletion?

- **Apprehension**—I see. And that helps, because—although it may not be apparent from the outline you reviewed—mastering the material in these sections is actually critical to the participants' achieving the goals you have for them. I realize it can be difficult to see that in the wording of the agenda.
- **Alternatives**—Recognizing you need to tighten the delivery time, are you open to my recommendations on how to tailor the content to meet your goals? Knowing the course, the learners' backgrounds that you shared, and what you defined as desired results, I would recommend looking at *X*, *Y*, and *Z* as content we can leave as reference material. I'd also suggest that *X* will not be as valuable to your team based on where they are right now.

Scenario 5. A senior manager in the department that does the most hiring tells you that the full-day NEO needs to be distilled to a half-day format but still cover all the existing content, because she needs the new hires operation-ready when they get to the warehouse floor after lunch. She shares that shouldn't be too hard if you cut out all the socializing components that are wasted time and just tell them what they need to know.

- **Appreciate**—You may or may not know that a passion of mine is working with newly hired staff, so I particularly appreciate being asked to look at this with you.
- **Acknowledge**—I understand your need to have an effective program that prepares new hires for their role.
- **Ask**—Will you describe for me what "operation-ready" will ideally look like?
- **Apprehension**—Okay, good. That is a bit less aggressive than I thought your answer might have been. I'm just concerned that if we cut the time so drastically, without prioritizing what to include and what to pare down, the learners will be drinking from a fire hose and take nothing away other than feeling overwhelmed. I remember my first day here—there was a lot to take in.
- **Alternatives**—I'd like to suggest that we look at the NEO from a fresh perspective. We might even want to change the name from new employee orientation—which almost implies a passive experience—to something more action- and

results-oriented—I'll brainstorm some ideas. Basically, instead of starting with what already exists in the course, I am suggesting we begin with what you want the training to achieve and let that guide the content. We might end up with a half-day training room event that is heavily focused on skill development versus presentation of content and an afternoon shadowing experience, partnering each new hire with one of your top performers out on the floor—as one possibility. Are you open to considering a few options before deciding?

Your own situation: What will be your plan to redefine the finish line of a request that may be unrealistic—or worse—not in the best interests of the learners?

Appreciate—

Acknowledge—

Ask—

Apprehension—

Alternatives—

Final Thoughts

When you say "yes" to everything—every request, every deliverable, every deadline, every bit of content—you are, in essence, saying "no" to the learners and to yourself. You are telling learners: no, I won't insulate you from misguided requests; no, I won't protect you from data dumps; no, I am not willing to defend your need for interactive learning experiences, to name a few. You are also saying no to yourself—to your experience, your industry expertise, your desire to design, develop, and deliver effective learning events you are proud of—and no to maintaining a work schedule that is manageable and allows you to accomplish all that you are capable of.

The Five A's are your tool to manage expectations. They give you a sequential process to follow to give learners what they need, generate results for project sponsors and the business, and allow you to bring your full value to your projects.

If your reaction to Chapter 1 is "That might work if I were brought in early on, but in my organization learning and development (L&D) is the last group to hear that someone wants training. By the time I get involved it is too late for the Five A's," then Chapter 2 is for you. Before moving into Chapter 2, work through the Put It Into Practice exercise below and review the Chapter Actions list, on the next page, to determine your next steps with this content.

Put It Into Practice

You just had a chance to apply the Five A's to your specific situation. Below, I encourage you to take a bigger picture view of the model (Appreciate, Acknowledge, Ask, Apprehension, Alternatives). Consider how your current project communications compare. Identify your strengths in relation to the model. Identify your blind spots too. Then use the space on the next page—or a notepad or tablet—to record your reactions to each column heading.

Continue	Stop	Start
Actions that align with the model that I will **continue** doing.	Actions that don't align with the model that I will **stop** doing.	Actions in the model that I will **start** doing.

Next, record three actions you will take to move you closer to where you want to be.

1. ______________________________
2. ______________________________
3. ______________________________

Chapter Actions

- ❑ Complete the three actions you identified in the Put It Into Practice activity.
- ❑ Assess your current level of performance with the Five A's, using the assessment instrument in Chapter 10.
- ❑ Revisit past projects to see where the Five A's could have helped you.
- ❑ Plan for your next project scoping meeting using the Five A's worksheet and job aid in Chapter 10.
- ❑ Use the chapter-by-chapter action plan in Chapter 10 to record any additional actions you will take based on the content of this chapter.

2

What If I Am the Last One to the Table?

The One Way to Earn a Seat, and Four Strategies to Get You There

If you are the last one to the table, you need to fix that. Quickly! Until you are at the table, you will be working at a disadvantage, your projects will be more challenging, and your effectiveness will be limited.

What Does Having a Seat at the Table Look Like?

Having a seat at the table simply means being present when decisions are being made—decisions that will influence the project you need to execute, decisions on the timelines you will be held to, decisions that create project constraints as well as expectations that you will be required to work within and rise to. I am sure you have your own stories of what was decided about training when you weren't present. I call these preexisting decisions. It also means having a voice in the discussions that drive the direction of learning projects, and it means being involved from inception. Sounds pretty nice, doesn't it? In Chapter 10, there is an Earning Your Seat at the Table worksheet. You may want to complete it now, before reading the rest of this chapter. It can inform your reading.

Getting to the Table

So, how does one obtain that coveted seat? The fortunate ones reading this are in organizations in which L&D is already recognized for the value its team brings and are wondering why this book needs a chapter on this, since their spot is already reserved. The rest of us have a few options (but only one is recommended—you are welcome to see it differently).

You could *whine*—complain that being brought in so late in the game places an undue burden on the team and that if last-minute requests continue to be standard, the team will burn out and training programs will suffer. You could *demand*—create a L&D policy that states projects will only be undertaken if the team is brought in at inception and all other project requests will be declined. You could *be "that person"*—keep an eye on the conference room, watch for a critical mass to form, and pop your head in to ask, "Hey, is something going on I should know about? I can grab a pen and be right back." Or, you could be *persuasive*—the recommended approach.

> Earning a seat at the table is the only meaningful way to get there. You could grumble until one is given, mandate one, or strong-arm your way into one. But it is only when you earn your seat that anyone else at the table listens when you speak.

My grandmother's adage "you attract more bees with honey than vinegar" also holds true with securing your seat. This story, from the start of my career (in a different job function), illustrates what persuasive can look like:

> A large insurance brokerage firm in Manhattan hired me as a communications specialist in their Professional Communications group when I graduated with a master's degree in journalism. My role was to write proposals for new business in response to requests for proposals—RFPs. The process, when I first started, involved many individuals from different parts of the company (property, casualty, marine, aviation, risk management, and others) drafting "their" sections and sending them to me to assemble into a single report a few days before it was due—when I was lucky. I was on salary, supporting sales teams that earned commissions.

I enjoyed the job, in part, because it was challenging. Challenging because drafts were commonly received days before submission deadlines—not leaving much time for me to do my best. Challenging because contributors wrote their sections as if they were the only section—and often contradicted one another. And, challenging because I always wanted to deliver the best possible product I could in the time available to me—and they weren't giving me enough. Therefore, there were Thursday mornings when I was at the copier wearing the same suit I arrived in on Wednesday, as well as late-night town car rides out of Manhattan after public transportation had stopped running to my station (long before ride-sharing apps).

But it wasn't always that way. After each RFP was finalized and shipped for overnight delivery to meet its deadline, I would apologize to the team lead that I was sorry it wasn't better. I'd say what I felt I had achieved in the time available to me, and then explain that if I had had more time I would have . . . [any number of things that may have put them in a better position to win the business—and earn their commission]. For example, "while the concept graphic we created is great because it tells the whole story in one view, I would have really liked to have had the time to break it into pieces as well and then integrate those images of the key components alongside the narrative that supports each." Or, "I was able to align their values with our risk management philosophy in the introduction, but I simply ran out of time to reinforce that point in Larry's mitigation section—I'm sorry." When the next RFP was issued, they would give me more time—and still I'd identify what I did well and apologize for what I didn't get to. For the next opportunity, they would bring me in even earlier; followed by another apology and value stack from me. After a few rounds of this, when an RFP arrived, I was invited to the initial strategy meetings. Getting a seat at the table required multiple steps, each getting me closer—but I earned my seat by both proving my value and expressing what additional value I could bring if given the opportunity.

Earning a seat, while hard work, is far different from grumbling until one is given, mandating one, or strong-arming your way into one (corporate musical chairs so to speak), because when you *earn* your seat, others around the table actually listen when you speak.

There are many reasons you want to be at the table. In the context of this book, it is so that you can make the shift from executing orders—like a glorified line cook—to guiding projects in a direction that improves the outcome—more like a concierge.

Thimble Stew

I liken this to making thimble stew—a story I recall from my childhood in which a child visits a miserly relative and asks if they can cook a pot of stew only to be told there is nothing in the house with which to make stew. The child replies that it won't be a problem, because thimble stew only needs water and any old thimble. With the water and thimble boiling on the stove, the child stirs the pot, sniffs at the steam, and comments at how nicely it is coming along. Then she adds that if they only had some onions, and maybe a carrot or two, it would be even better. At the thought of an even better meal, the miserly relative goes into the storage room and returns with both. Stirring and chopping, the child comments that on one occasion beans were added, making it tastier. The relative replies there might be a can of beans around—if they look hard for them. And so it goes with a growing list of ingredients that would make the final dish more delicious, until a full pot of savory stew is bubbling on the stove.

Here are four strategies for making "training thimble stew" and better positioning yourself for future projects. We will look at each in turn:

- ✓ Leverage your current projects.
- ✓ Leverage your champions.
- ✓ Leverage your proposals.
- ✓ Leverage your relationships.

Leverage Your Current Projects

This is the approach I used in my insurance career in Manhattan, as you saw in my story. It wasn't intentional at the time—but it can be for you. Only in recent years, as instructional designers in my classes asked how to get stakeholders to seek out their expertise, how to become involved from the start, and how to get out from behind the order-taker window, did I see with hindsight's clarity how critical it is.

The technique packages two elements together. It begins with a statement of accomplishment—something you did well in the finished product. Even better, something you did *very* well. That is followed by what you would have done and wished you'd had the time to do for them—and apologizing that it didn't occur on *this* project. If you balk at the idea of "apologizing"—after all, it's not your fault they didn't have the forethought to include you earlier—recognize it does several things for you. This approach highlights your accomplishments, shows that you have even more to offer, demonstrates you are willing to take responsibility for outcomes, and says you would like to be able to deliver even better results . . . *for them* . . . if only they would help you to help them.

Here are a few examples taken from the world of training. You will see that the "apology" element can be direct, soft, or inferred:

- "I am really pleased with how the custom case studies came together. The managers who reviewed them said they are incredibly relatable and represent the challenges their employees are facing. Had we had time to create branched scenarios though—such as a build-your-own-adventure book—the learners would have been able to receive targeted feedback as they made decisions. Let's plan to consider that on a future project where we have more lead time. I'm just sorry we weren't able to do it for this course."
- "Given our timeline, we didn't really have the luxury of considering other delivery formats, and although the face-to-face design is receiving excellent evaluations, it isn't surprising the data also shows learners would have preferred this in an e-learning format. I realize the decision was made before I was involved—it is just a shame when we miss an opportunity to align with our customers' preferences."
- "Based on initial feedback, 85 percent of the participants indicate that the videos we sourced and integrated improved their retention. Wouldn't it have been great for us to shoot our own videos?

They would have been less expensive and could have been completely customized to our sales model. We just ran out of time with the hard stop required to rollout the program at the sales conference. Please know it is never too soon to let me know you foresee a training need."

- "I'll be honest—as proud as I am of what we built in the time we had, I really would have liked to integrate job-embedded activities into the course design. I know we didn't have the time for it on this project. It is just that I also know how beneficial the integrated model is to helping learners transfer the skills from the training room back to the job."

What can you say to leverage your work on a current project to better position yourself on future projects?

- Accomplishment Statement: ______________________________
  ____

  PLUS
- Apology for what wasn't done (due to time constraints, preexisting decisions, or such):
  ____
  ____

Leverage Your Champions

Are there select projects on which you were brought in early? For which your perspective, expertise, and recommendations were sought? That resulted in significant successes for the sponsor? Chances are these projects were requested or led by champions of learning who are likely the same people you called after reading the beginning of Chapter 1. Let your successes with them pave the way to similar successes in other parts of the organization or with other clients.

Remember to seek permission from your champions to reference their projects—and more important, their results. Also, keep your champions informed when you use this strategy. Right or wrong, some clients will place greater priority on a message received from a peer of theirs than from you. When your champions know the field you are playing on, their cheers over the successes achieved with you are more likely to be heard!

When you are at the table, contributing to the development of the solution and weighing in on the pros and cons of options, the outcome will be real results. Use this four-step formula to help others see what your champions already know and get yourself to the table:

- ✓ Step 1: Make a connection between the new request and the champion's project.
- ✓ Step 2: Differentiate the new request from the champion's project.
- ✓ Step 3: Deliver the good news of what you can do for the requestor.
- ✓ Step 4: Ask for the invitation to the table.

Step 1: Make a connection between the new request and the champion's project.

Draw inspiration from these sample phrases. As you review them, replace the *X* and *Y* blanks so that *X* = the name of the champion or his project and *Y* = a project detail from the current request.

- "Like your situation, *X* needed *Y*."
- "This request reminds me of a project I completed with *X*. He also *Y*."
- "Listening to you, I am reminded of a successful project I worked on with *X*. There are multiple commonalities, including *Y*, *Y*, and *Y*."

Step 2: Differentiate the new request from the champion's project.

Because your intent is to earn a seat at the table going forward, emphasize the disparity in project schedule, opportunity to consult on the training plan, extent of advance notice, project deadlines and so on.

- "A key difference in that project was . . .
  - — the training team was involved a bit earlier—quite a bit actually—and we were able to make recommendations on the complete solution."
  - — because we were brought in early, we were able to *Y*, *Y*, and *Y*."
  - — we had significant development time, which allowed more opportunity to get creative."

Step 3: Deliver the good news.

After Step 2, your current project requestor may be feeling a bit downtrodden; as if it is too late for him to have a successful initiative too. It is important to assure him that he will also have a positive result. It may just be refined in scope compared to the champion's program.

- "But here is the good news, we are connecting now, and . . .
  - — we *can* create some support tools for you."
  - — I agree there is a training need."
  - — with the timeline we *do* have, we can certainly *Y*."
- "I have some good news to share . . .
  - — here is what I see that we *can* successfully accomplish with the time we have."
  - — I think a phased approach may buy us some time. Phase One would align with your current schedule and launch in 30 days. I am envisioning *Y* for Phase One, with subsequent phases spaced out 45 to 60 days after the previous one. These phases could include *Y*, *Y*, and even *Y*. What are your thoughts on a multi-phased model?"
  - — although it is not our preferred way to work, the training team has met similarly aggressive schedules in the past. We will get this done for you, the project scope may just need to be a bit narrower than I would have liked for you. Know that the core elements and sound instructional design principles will be there; we may just need to leave out some of the extras this time."

Step 4: Ask for the invitation to the table.

Although it may be apparent to you that you are using the first three steps to establish the value of being brought in early, it may not be as obvious to the person who did not invite you in earlier. For this reason, Step 4 is critical. Asking to be invited can't be so direct as to appear gauche or confrontational. You don't want to be an unwelcome guest invited out of guilt or awkwardness, and you certainly don't want a turf war. Bottom line: You want to be invited because the project sponsor recognizes the value you bring.

Consider how any of the following phrases may work for you, and modify them to fit your needs:

- "Going forward, give me a call as soon as you even suspect there may be a training need. I will be in an even stronger position to support you that way."
- "Just a thought . . . if we connect quarterly and talk about what initiatives are taking place in your department, the training team and I can start blocking project time for your needs. Would you like that?"
- "Please know that the more informed the training team is on what you are working on, the better we will be able to support you. Never hesitate to bring us in to consult—that is why we are here."
- "We both are now better informed for the next learning need—and I will look forward to getting started on that one with you from inception! Thank you so much for your collaborative attitude today."

Leverage Your Proposals

Raise your hand if you always want to do the *most* you can for the learners who attend your programs. And raise your other hand if that holds true even when unrealistic project constraints are imposed on you. Now, pick up the book—because my money is on you having dropped it when you placed both hands in the air! As often as I hear frustrations over what training is expected to accomplish, I more often hear them about the timelines training is expected to be delivered within.

To stay true to your commitment to your work, you will either need to rein in the expectations with your proposals when the project timeline is a fixed variable or leverage your proposals to gain more design and development time—or perhaps both. Sometimes, when a client sees what they could have—if only certain resources were available—they will want it enough to make those resources available . . . thimble stew! Whether the resources are learners' time (class length), development time (project timeline), financial support, or all of these and more.

Here is how it can work. Choose three timeframes. The first will be the amount of time "given" to you when the project is assigned, delegated, or requested. Let's call that one month for our example. The second will be a more comfortable timeframe for you that also accounts for the requested timeline—a bit of a compromise between what the requestor asked for and your ideal. Maybe 45 days. The third is your ideal timeframe—the amount of time that is actually needed to do all the work (and "all the work" includes the elements discussed in Chapters 5, 6, and 7). Does 90 days sound about right? Or 120 days? More? The timeframes can vary widely based on the request.

Next, for each timeframe, outline a different set of deliverables. This might take a basic, classic, best-in-class approach, as in the first example in Figure 2-1, with expanded deliverables for each incremental increase in design and development time. Or, each proposed timeline can take a fundamentally different approach to the learning solution, and therefore come with different deliverables, as in the second example.

The beauty of this approach is that it can help you now *and* on future projects. For your current project, you will be able to give it your all—toward a contained deliverable. You may even find this approach buys you more time when the requestor sees what more you could do for them with the additional time. Going forward, this internal or external client will realize that if you have more development time, you can do more for them.

> Stop letting the tail wag the dog. Plan your annual project calendar. Then fit last-minute requests around your planned projects (if you can accommodate them) instead of the other way around.

Leverage Your Relationships

Good things come to those who wait—but great things come to those who go out and make it happen.

FIGURE 2-1. SAMPLE DESIGN AND DEVELOPMENT TIMELINES

Timeline 1 Project Deliverables		
30 Days	**45 Days**	**90 Days**
• Interactive course design • Participant materials • Visual aids • Facilitator outline	• Interactive course design • Participant materials • Visual aids • Facilitator guide with scripting • Job aid • Ghost-written emails	• Interactive course design • Participant materials • Visual aids • Facilitator guide with scripting and embedded answer keys • Manipulatives for in-class activities • Job aid • Ghost-written emails aligned with a communication campaign • Assessments • Manager support tools • Train-the-trainer option

Timeline 2 Project Approaches		
30 Days	**45 Days**	**120 Days**
Source or create a set of self-paced instructional aids for learners to access and complete independently. Assessment will be integrated by posing self-reflection questions and providing action planning worksheets to be completed at the learners' discretion.	Build an e-learning module with interactive features and assessments built in that will include scenario-based activities that use "build-your-own-adventure" branching to allow for exploration and tailored feedback. Knowledge gain will be assessed via an in-course assessment using multiple choice and true/false questions.	Develop a blended-learning solution that uses a flipped classroom model. Video-based instruction and self-assessment tools will be completed independently. Then, small groups will attend ILT sessions to work through application exercises and receive one-on-one feedback. Job-embedded application assignments will be required components that learners complete as they apply the skills in the workplace and receive feedback and coaching from their instructor.

Simply put, stop waiting for the phone to ring and start making calls. When you are in responsive mode—taking on projects as requests are made—it is difficult to prioritize projects, manage effective project timelines, dedicate time to negotiating the best deliverables, and ensure your efforts are focused on the most important projects.

When you are so busy working to fulfill requests that you can't slow down long enough to assess the merits of requests being made or determine the best strategies to achieve their goals you probably are not putting out your best work either. And less than your best perpetuates the Vicious Cycle of not being valued, which leads to not getting invited to the table, which leads to your expertise not factoring into training solutions, which leads to receiving additional requests that may be misguided. In other words, the tail wagging the dog.

Instead, get ahead of requests by developing open lines of communication with key managers, department heads, project managers, and so on. Based on their input and anticipated training needs, plan your project calendar. Yes, plan your design and development schedule and fit last-minute requests around your project plan—if they can be accommodated at all—instead of the other way around.

Turn away requests? Yes! For many learning professionals this is a very difficult concept. Before giving up on the idea as too uncomfortable, think about how this plays out in three food service models (see Figure 2-2).

Where do you begin to leverage relationships so that you can gain—or regain—control of your work? As you would with any challenge—from where you are. If you already have a full workload for the next month, three months, or six months, begin planning what projects you will take on two, four, or seven months out. Know that when that date arrives, you will be in control of your design time and working more effectively at a more relaxed pace. Here's how:

- **Start by looking back at the past year's projects.** Who was easiest to work with? Most collaborative? More concerned with achieving results than checking a box? Reach out to them and ask what upcoming needs they envision. If you are planning your project calendar, why not start by making space for those who want to do training the right way and are a pleasure to work with?

Figure 2-2. Three Models From the Restaurant Industry

Model 1: The BBQ Joint

Down the street from my neighborhood there is a bare-bones barbeque joint. Six days a week, the scent of pulled pork, chicken, and ribs wafts from the building in billows of smoke. Every day, staff arrive and prepare the same items as the day before in the same quantities. Every year the place wins an award for being the best—at doing one thing, BBQ. Customers queue up in long lines, place orders for what they want—or what is left—and when the food runs out everyone goes home.

Model 2: Chain Restaurant

There are also many national chain restaurants in my area. Their food is consistent, if not inspired. Most nights they are packed. Hostesses take names and hand out beepers. Line cooks sauté, broil, and plate furiously. Wait staff get in the weeds. Service and quality suffer. When meals are served, it isn't uncommon that the order is wrong, and because everyone is so busy, correcting it can be a challenge.

Model 3: Upscale Restaurant

An upscale restaurant sits at the edge of my neighborhood too. If you want visiting houseguests to experience their blueberry and corn salad or any number of other delights, you had better make a reservation. Because once they have made commitments to deliver their best to the customers who notified them they were coming, they turn away additional customers—for that night anyway—and the next-available reservation will be offered.

What Does This Mean for Your Training Projects?

In comparison to these three restaurant models, how do you want to be known? As the learning professional who delivers a great product—as long as customers like the one thing you make and haven't already had enough of it? As the learning professional who works frenetically to meet demand and turns out a product that is, at best, preferable to the customer making their own? Or as the learning professional who is dedicated to producing quality over quantity and who will tailor customers' products to their particular needs, restrictions, and preferences—leaving them singing your praises to everyone who will listen?

- **Next, look at organizational initiatives.** Will the company be pursuing awards, credentialing, or certifications? Who will be driving these initiatives and how might training support achieving these goals? Who in your network can connect you to the people behind these projects? Get in touch and start blocking the time they will need.
- **Find your underserved populations.** Most organizations have one or more groups whose learning needs are neglected. Perhaps they are geographically removed, their functions don't generate revenue, they have experienced tremendous turnover in their management, or any number of other reasons that leave them at the back of the pack. Who can tell you what their needs are and what they will most value? Decide where they will fit in your plan.
- **Connect with the leaders who make things happen and get things done**—the ones who have big ideas and garner the attention of decision makers. What are their current goals, pet projects, or unfulfilled needs? Which of your champions have access to this group and can get you a meeting? What are their key dates?

> **Insider Tip**
>
> Establish a learning council. Invite a cross-section of leaders, managers, high-potentials, and frontline performers to participate. With this diverse group of stakeholders, get strategic about the training being created and implemented instead of remaining reactive.

By tapping into these four groups, you increase your odds of creating a schedule that includes four essentials: fun projects, high-profile projects, deeply appreciated projects, and projects that people will be talking about. This cross-section of work will get your projects noticed for all the right reasons. Working with you will become something everyone values, and that, in turn, will result in work units making reservations to work with you as well as asking for the chef's recommendations!

Final Thoughts

To be relevant, to be your most effective, to do your best work, you need to be at the table when decisions are being made. What is your plan to get there? How will you make training thimble stew?

If you are not at the table, you are likely working incredibly hard to fulfill requests. Shifting that effort forward—and putting in the work required to earn your seat—will enable you to cultivate the training culture in your organization and set the bar to which your clients hold external vendors. You can get to the table, and be heard once there, by leveraging your current projects, champions, proposals, and relationships.

Put It Into Practice

Here is the table. Where are you? Draw an X to indicate where are you in relation to "the table"?

If you are not *at* the table . . . what actions are you going to take to get there?

1.
2.
3.

(Note: The further away you are, the more critical your action ideas and notes will be.)

Chapter Actions

- ❑ Complete the three actions you just listed in the Put It Into Practice activity.
- ❑ Revisit past projects to see where Chapter 2 strategies could have helped you. Plan key points in your current projects to use the strategies.
- ❑ Determine who your champions are.
- ❑ Set your strategy for planning your project development schedule.
- ❑ Schedule meetings or calls with target learning council members to gain their support and input for the council structure, goals, and so on.
- ❑ Revisit your chapter-by-chapter action plan in Chapter 10 and update it with actions related to the content of this chapter.

3

Whose Needs Do I Put First?

30+ Strategies to Put Learners First Without Alienating Project Sponsors

The learners' needs must come first. When they don't, learners disconnect during training, learning doesn't occur, new behaviors aren't realized, and the whole project is an effort in futility.

But there can be tension here, between the learners' needs and the sponsors' requests. The training professional's job is to stand in that gap and create the best training possible for both the learner and the sponsoring organization.

It can be easy to get caught up in pleasing the project sponsors. They're your clients after all and may even be your boss. How they assess the experience of working with you will have ramifications for you and your career now and in the future. It is understandable to want to say "yes" to them.

But a "yes" to misguided requests will achieve compromised results and training programs that don't accomplish their goals. Typically, the blame for that will fall on you—and, honestly, it should. If you recognize a request to be misguided, and do nothing to redirect it, you are complicit—you knew better and did nothing to stop it.

As instructional designers and trainers, you are the first and second lines of defense for learners. Learners rely on you to look out for their interests in training. And the surest way to prioritize your learners is to skillfully manage your sponsors. This chapter provides more than 30 strategies, in three categories, to get you there. First, though, let's look at why we need to be savvy with our sponsors—why it isn't enough for me to simply tell you to prioritize the learners' needs over the clients' requests.

Client Turned Adversary

A strange phenomenon can take place in the business partner/learning professional relationship. At least it seems strange until you think about it for a moment—and then it is quite logical.

Let's look at how the relationship often unfolds. The business unit has a need. Training is deemed the solution to the problem. You are then called in to "do what you do" to address the problem. From the sponsor's point of view, you are a resource to fulfill a need—a need he has outlined for you. As you discuss the need, his envisioned solution, and the influencing factors, and then share the importance of assessing his need, a shift can occur. Now, instead of moving his problem toward its solution, you are creating a new problem for him. You have stopped his forward momentum because you are questioning his envisioned solution. You have just challenged him—game on.

Now, it may not be as harsh as "game on," but when you ask him to see you as a partner instead of a resource, when you raise questions he may not have considered, and when you suggest talking to additional stakeholders to get a full and objective view of the situation, the sponsor can easily feel second-guessed and threatened.

Instead of being his resource—and you certainly are not yet his partner—you may be judged an adversary. This may only be happening at a subconscious level for the sponsor, but without a doubt it is happening.

What Your Client May Be Thinking

"Are you going to make me look bad?"

"Will you set back my schedule to roll out a solution?"

"What will my boss say when you (some guy from L&D!) say we need something other than what I suggested at last week's meeting?"

"Will people see me as little more than a figurehead?"

"Are you going to put me over budget on this?"

"What are you going to say about me to my team *if* I let you talk with them?"

"Are you going to take credit for fixing this when I was the one that brought you in?"

Adversary Turned Champion

Protecting the interests—needs—of the learners will be much easier for you to do with the project sponsor on your side. Working with him will always be easier than working against him. It is in your best interests, and your learners', for you to do all you can to ensure a potentially rivalrous relationship becomes a *partnership*. I'll go further—you must do all you can to convert a potential adversary into one of your champions. And you can do that using these three categories of strategies:

- ✓ Request warm transfers.
- ✓ Keep the project sponsor informed.
- ✓ Give the project sponsor the limelight.

Request Warm Transfers

The first strategy for converting sponsors into champions may be the easiest recommendation in this book: Request warm transfers. To conduct an effective needs analysis, you are going to need to speak with additional people, look at existing data, gather new data, and more. That will require access to people and information. Instead of cold-calling people or mass distributing surveys in hopes of responses, ask the project sponsor to open doors for you. Warm transfers are effective for many reasons:

- They keep the project sponsor at the forefront.
- They grant you the sponsor's permission to connect with these people (which maintains the power balance he might fear you threaten).
- They leverage his clout to your advantage. People will more readily take your calls, accept your meeting requests, and reply to your surveys. You will become a priority to them because the project sponsor is a priority to them.

Besides simply asking "Can you make warm transfers to these people for me?," there are several techniques you can use to enhance warm transfers:

- Ghost-write an email the sponsor can send to introduce you and your role in helping him address a need.
- Provide the sponsor with a few talking points to address if he prefers to make warm transfers by phone or in person. These points will be the same elements you would have included in the email: what project he has brought you in to assist on, your role in the initiative, what his expectations are of the person he is connecting you with, how the initiative will benefit that person, and so on.
- Prepare any survey instruments and cover emails to be sent under the project sponsor's name.
- When you contact the people the sponsor connects you to, tell them he asked you to reach out.

Keep the Project Sponsor Informed

A second way to convert sponsors from adversaries to champions is to keep your sponsor informed during the analysis phase of a project—while you are determining needs, assessing what skill and knowledge gaps may exist, and so on. Your sponsor will feel as if he is part of the process and won't get any unwanted surprises. Be sure to share your activity schedule with your sponsor and include the following information:

- With whom you have lined up meetings and when they are scheduled
- The date you are planning to conduct your focus group, who has agreed to attend, and the format you intend to follow
- When surveys will be distributed
- What reports and data you are requesting from his team and others in the organization
- Other activities you are planning so that your sponsor is fully informed

If the sponsor isn't concerned about this level of detail, he will tell you. Err on the side of too much information rather than not enough.

Keeping your sponsor informed on what your analysis yielded will be fairly straightforward when your findings are consistent with or closely aligned to his initial request: "Good news Matt, you were right!"

How Would You Handle It?

Matt came to you with a preexisting decision. His team will be attending a three-day industry conference in a few months, which presents significant networking and lead generating opportunities for them, and he has decided to attach a training session to it to save travel expenses. He is flexible on the timing—either the day before or the day after the conference.

When you connect with the intended learners, you find they don't share Matt's enthusiasm. Yes, they would like the training opportunity, but the timing is all wrong. They cite conflicting priorities if training is the day after the conference—that is when they will be following through on commitments made at the conference and working to build their network of new contacts from the event. When asked about scheduling training the day before the conference, they quickly point out that, this year, the conference follows a holiday weekend and they are not eager to cut their vacation time short to come to a class.

How can you respect Matt's position and authority while gently leading him to alternatives that will meet his staff's learning needs better?

It can be more challenging for you, however, when there is a disconnect between his request and what the analysis shows to be the true need. In these instances, frame the information you gathered in the context of what you learned in your initial conversation with the sponsor (which was guided by the Five A's of Chapter 1).

Open the discussion with the findings from your analysis that align with his request—even if only marginally. You can then segue into the conflicting findings. Consider how the following phrasing can work for you:

- "In our first conversation, you shared *X* was a priority. Here are the items the focus group raised that are aligned with that priority. . . ."
- "I know it was critical to you that *X*, and the team agrees—with one minor modification. . . ."
- "Interestingly, the survey respondents did not place a high value on *X* as we thought they would."
- "Some surprising findings we didn't anticipate—but which I see as critical—are. . . ."

If met with resistance, you might consider redirecting the discussion using one of these ideas:

- "I hear where you are coming from. My only concern is this. . . ."
- "I certainly recognize the constraints of the project; if there is one thing that I'd suggest is critical in these findings above everything else, it is. . . ."
- "Among the people you put me in contact with, there was overwhelming agreement that *X* will present a real challenge to operations. I wouldn't be doing my job if I didn't stress this now, as I believe it will have a significant impact on how the training is received."
- "My concern is that we have asked for their input and, based on where we are right now, it looks as though we are not integrating any of it. I'm just not sure how that will go over."
- "Certainly, the final decision is yours; I am just thinking about what you said early on about how critical it is to have everyone's buy-in on this."

- "Would you like to give this input from the group some thought before we make a final decision? I can get started on other aspects of the project in the meantime."

At later stages of the project—such as design and development—you will still want to keep the sponsor informed, but in different ways. When you are designing the solution, don't assume the sponsor will see the rationale of your design choices. This is a great opportunity to create teachable moments that can enhance the sponsor's awareness of adult learning principles and thereby transition him to being a champion of learning (and of yours). Walk him through the logic of your sequencing. Highlight a few of the adult learning principles (see Chapter 8) that influenced how you structured an activity. Show him how, through guided discovery, learners will arrive at a predefined outcome and how participants will receive targeted feedback at key points. The better he can see why you have done what you have done in the design, the less likely he will be to want to change it.

Equally true, as you move into the development phase, don't just send drafts of templates you created and intend to use after he approves them. Instead, schedule a meeting to review the templates together. Explain your choices for using photos instead of clip art, for limiting the number of fonts used in workbooks and visuals to two, why minimal text and complementing visuals are the mainstay of slides, and so on. When you proactively inform the sponsor of the reasons for your choices, he can assess them in that light. If you don't share these insights and he wants to make changes based on preferences, you are back to the "his opinion vs. your opinion" dilemma mentioned in Chapter 1.

Give the Project Sponsor the Limelight

The third strategy for turning sponsors into champions—and thus enabling you to put your learners' needs first—is to make sure you make the sponsor look good. And do it at every opportunity you have.

When you get comfortable giving away credit, an interesting thing happens: People enjoy working with you. Cynics may say "of course they do—they are getting the credit," but the savvy will recognize that if you are the common factor among all the projects that people are receiving credit for, your role in the successes will not go unnoticed. You will shine brightly because everyone you support shines. And, in the end, which is brighter? A single beam shining on you, or the light of many beams reflecting on you?

Now, there are individuals who will accept credit like a black hole. Not only will they prevent any credit from reflecting back on you, they will claim ownership of your ideas and strategies and may even believe the ideas were their own. In my experience, a person who does that does it consistently, which means other people recognize the behavior. Don't worry about the black holes. You may even choose to recognize it as a form of flattery if you're feeling especially gracious.

Making the sponsor look good makes it much easier for you to keep the learners' needs at the forefront. When the sponsor trusts you, trusts that you won't undermine him, trusts that he doesn't need to keep a watchful eye over what you do, who you talk to, and what you say to them, he will give you much more latitude for your work. Consider these ideas to give credit away and place the project sponsor in the limelight—with sincerity:

- During scoping conversations (Chapter 1), listen for and make note of areas of agreement. Later in the project, say things like "Matt had a great idea to . . . ," instead of "Matt and I agreed it would be best to. . . ."
- Compliment the sponsor's behaviors, ideas, project support, and so on when he *isn't* present. He may expect you to defer to him and speak well of him when he is in the room, but he will place more importance on what he learns through the grapevine regarding how you speak of him in his absence.
- Mention the project sponsor, by name, in emails you draft for managers to send to program participants before they participate in training (see Chapter 5). Credit him for creating the training opportunity and how it benefits the participants.
- Acknowledge the project sponsor, by name, in the printed participant materials you develop.

- When your work is complimented, express your appreciation and then mention a contribution from the project sponsor that made your accomplishments possible.
- Create moments to acknowledge his collaborative approach, trust in the instructional design process, prioritization of the project in the face of competing demands, and the like in the presence of his boss, director, peers, and others who matter to him.

Final Thoughts

If you are caught up in turf wars with project sponsors, they can quickly and easily restrict your access to the people and information critical to your work. Avoid that by intentionally winning them over.

When you implement the strategies in Chapter 3 well and with sincerity, everyone will get what they want. You will enjoy working on a project that adds value and has meaning to the organization. Participants learn skills that are relevant to and align with their needs. The business achieves its desired outcomes—which can only happen when the participants commit themselves to developing the new skills and applying them. And when the project sponsor realizes a success, he comes out the hero.

Manage this balancing act—of putting learners first and converting sponsors into champions—poorly, and it may be your last chance to design for this learner group. Manage it well and you have given yourself the best PR possible.

Put It Into Practice

Rate your current level of effectiveness at consistently demonstrating the three strategies in this chapter by placing marks along each scale on the next page that align with your current reality. Then identify the actions you will take to improve your ratings—there is always room for improvement in this arena!

Requesting warm transfers

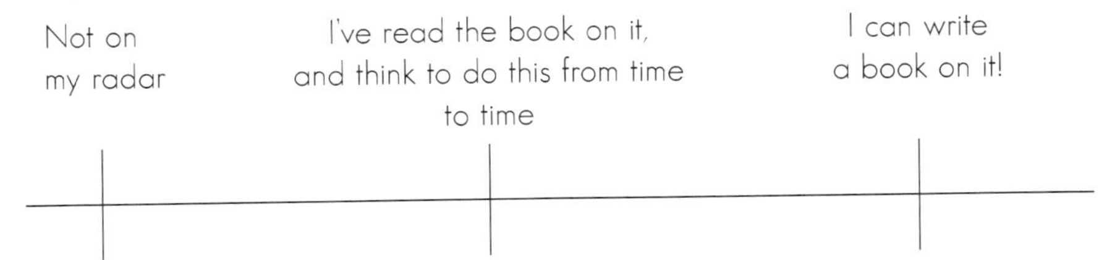

What I will do to improve my rating:
1.

2.

Keeping the project sponsor informed

Not on my radar

I've read the book on it, and think to do this from time to time

I can write a book on it!

What I will do to improve my rating:
1.

2.

Giving the project sponsor the limelight

Not on my radar

I've read the book on it, and think to do this from time to time

I can write a book on it!

What I will do to improve my rating:
1.

2.

Chapter Actions

- ❑ Take action on the improvement plans you listed in the Put It Into Practice activity.
- ❑ Draft a warm transfer email template that you can edit to tailor to new project requests as they are received.
- ❑ Edit the agenda template you follow for project kick-off meetings to include requesting warm transfers.
- ❑ Establish communication protocols during initial project meetings, including such agreements as email cc etiquette, format and timing of progress reports or briefings, and such.
- ❑ Make a conscious effort to look for and acknowledge ways in which the project sponsor advanced the project or supported its success.
- ❑ Revisit your chapter-by-chapter action plan in Chapter 10 and update it with actions related to the content of this chapter.

4

What Content Is Essential?

How to Identify Vital Content Using Two Powerful Questions

Knowing how to quickly and efficiently determine which content is essential is an important skill to master. The powerful questions and techniques in this chapter are your go-to tools in deciding what to keep and what to cut. The short answer to the question this chapter title poses is: It depends.

What is essential for a surfing trip to Cocoa Beach? For a trip to watch the Iditarod in Alaska? For hiking the Appalachian Trail? Clearly, choosing what is needed for travel depends on where you are going. For training events, it is much the same. It depends on where you want learners to end up and what the organization wants to achieve. In a nutshell, to know what to include, we need to know what success will look like.

Chapter 4 includes three discrete elements that will help you get to the essential content quickly and easily:

- ✓ An exercise to develop empathy for the challenge of distilling valuable content into vital content.
- ✓ A story to reiterate the point.
- ✓ A powerful two-question method to determine essential content.

Distilling Valuable Content Into Vital Content

Choose any topic—automotive repair, Argentine tango, a bibliography. Then perform an Internet search on the topic with the phrase "how to do" in front of it to see how much related content is available. In your pages of results, I am willing to bet there is nonessential content you quickly skip over, a tremendous amount of valuable material you might want to wade through if you had the time, and a smaller number of resources that are *vital* to your effective performance in relation to the topic. For example, although it might be *valuable* to compare variations in the Modern Language Association, American Psychological Association, and *Chicago Manual of Style* guides for bibliography creation, what is *vital* to your effective performance in writing one is knowing what data to collect and how to structure your bibliography based on the style guide followed by your organization. Valuable content is just that—it has value. But vital content is essential.

> The reason employees need to know things is so that they can *do* something with that knowledge. What do you need the leaners to be able to *do*?

To determine vital content, the desired outcome of the training must be identified first. There is a common challenge in this, however, which is revealed in Riley's story that follows:

> Riley, an instructional designer, was working with John, an influential department manager, to compress an existing supervisory skills program. In preparation for their initial scoping meeting, she reviewed the current curriculum, researched supervisory programs with alternative delivery formats, and developed a list of the skills addressed in the multiple courses. Early in their meeting, Riley suggested they begin by identifying the topics to include in the revised course so she could "work backwards" to tighten the timeframe, and John agreed. Great!

She handed John the list of skills including coaching, delegating, time management, mentoring, writing performance appraisals, progressive discipline, budgeting, feedback, onboarding new employees, compliance with federal employment regulations, preventing a hostile work environment, written and verbal business communications, safety, and more. Riley expected John to indicate which were critical to keep and which could be eliminated. John reviewed the list, and said, "That looks about right, our supervisors need all of these things. Oh, and let's add interviewing skills since there have been some recent problems with the hiring process . . . and maybe how to lead exit interviews too."

As you consider Riley's dilemma and the parallels in her situation with one you face, let's do a short exercise. Then we will revisit her story and your challenge of identifying what content is essential.

An Exercise in Empathy

Values play an essential role in our lives. They drive decisions. They determine compatibility with friends and relationships. They are at the core of who we are. Which values are dear to you? Figure 4-1 on the next page lists 55 values. The list isn't exhaustive, so add your own words as needed for the exercise.

Imagine you are going on a trip—the trip of life—and are traveling by plane. Your luggage allowance is one suitcase and one carry-on. Which values are most essential to take forward on your journey? Review the list, add or adjust words as needed, and choose your top 10. Write the values you will pack in the space provided.

FIGURE 4-1. VALUES

Achievement	Ethics	Integrity	Reliable
Altruism	Faith	Intelligence	Respectful
Authenticity	Fame	Joy	Responsible
Balance	Family	Justice	Risk
Beauty	Financial security	Kindness	Safety
Calm	Fitness	Leadership	Service
Community	Friendship	Learning	Success
Compassion	Generosity	Love	Teaching
Courage	Gratitude	Organization	Tenacity
Creativity	Happiness	Peace	Truthfulness
Dependable	Health	Positivity	________
Education	Honor	Power	________
Emotional well-being	Humility	Professional	________
Empathy	Inclusion	Provider	________
Equitable	Influence	Relationships	________

10 VALUES

1. ______________________________

2. ______________________________

3. ______________________________

4. ______________________________

5. ______________________________

6. ______________________________

7. ______________________________

8. ______________________________

9. ______________________________

10. ______________________________

How did that feel? Was it difficult to choose only 10? Did you find it easy and gravitate directly to certain words? You may have even decided to select 12 and gamble that the airline agent wouldn't notice your luggage was overweight! How did your challenge in choosing values compare to John's challenge of choosing training topics?

Knowing which 10 are critical to you may be comforting. But, what if you received a travel advisory before leaving home stating that due to a baggage handlers' strike, there will be no checked luggage on your flight? You will be allowed one carry-on though, which accommodates 5 values. Which 5 of your top 10 values would you place in your carry-on because they are that essential to you?

Write your list of 5 values on the facing page.

5 VALUES

1. ____________________

2. ____________________

3. ____________________

4. ____________________

5. ____________________

Whether or not choosing 10 was challenging, cutting the list in half likely was.

So, you are at the airport, carry-on in hand, and over the loudspeaker the gate agent makes an announcement. There has been a change in aircraft for your flight. Everyone does have a seat, but it is a smaller plane. The good news is that you can still bring one carry-on; however, due to space restrictions your bag can only hold 3 items.

Please open your carry-on and choose the 3 values you will be selecting to bring onboard.

Write your list of 3 values on the facing page.

3 VALUES

1. ______________________________

2. ______________________________

3. ______________________________

You began with a list of 55 provided ideas, and an endless list of your own thoughts on values, and have now boarded your flight with 3 values in a carry-on. Would it have seemed an insurmountable challenge to start off by selecting only 3?

You will be happy to know that the flight took off with you and your 3 values onboard—no new travel advisories to share. However, after a bit of unexpected turbulence causing a gauge to fail, the pilot announces, "In an abundance of caution, the plane will be making an emergency landing, please follow the direction of your flight attendant." The attendant's voice directs all passengers to prepare for a safe and orderly deplaning by grabbing two items, one in each hand—you must take your safety vest with one hand and use the other to take a single item from your carry-on. Which value do you choose?

Write your selected value here.

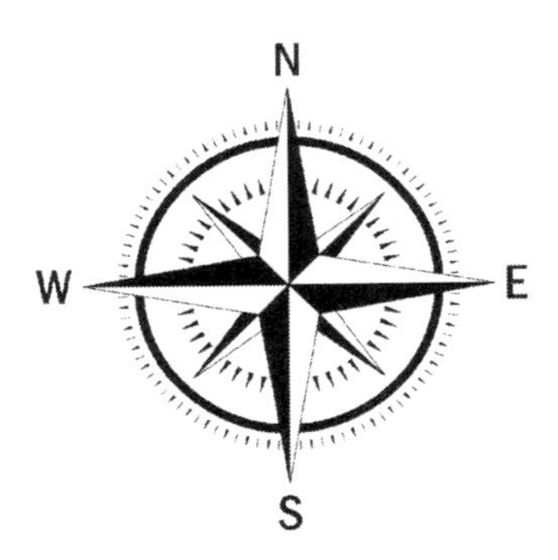

What did you take away from this exercise? Do you have a new perspective on John's dilemma? What about Riley's? Have you developed empathy for how difficult it can be to reduce *valuable* content to *vital* content?

Many people actually struggle selecting their first 10 values. Consider the extent of the challenge Riley presented to John.

A Story to Highlight John's Challenge

Instead of leading you through that exercise, I could have shared a brief story that parallels Riley and John's situation. The story goes like this:

> Having bought a home, my boyfriend at the time and I were preparing to paint the family room. After gathering no less than three dozen paint chips, I was getting nowhere in reducing the pile to my favorites. My boyfriend said, "Let me make this easy." He then picked up two samples and held them in front of me: "Which of these two do you like better?" I considered them both and selected the one in his left hand. He said, "Great,"—and then threw the one in his right hand over his shoulder, indicating it was clearly out of the running. He replaced that chip with a random choice from the pile on the table and asked again: "Which of *these* two do you like better?" And so the process continued until we were down to two choices, and "Interlude" won the battle of the paint chips. A lovely shade of tan.

Clearly, this story required less space in these pages than the activity. Equally true, I am confident you read it more quickly than you worked through the activity. Therefore, it might seem logical—in an effort to shorten the book and your time reading it—that I should have dropped the activity and just told the story. How often do you do that with your course designs? In an effort to meet the time constraint, you choose to fit more content into less time by replacing *doing with telling*. So why didn't I delete the activity? Why did I include both the activity and the story? These are not rhetorical questions. Why do you think I made these choices? Can you come up with one reason? Three? Five? Record them here:

Here are my reasons. I want you to experience John's challenge. I want you to walk in his shoes and develop empathy for how hard it can be to let go of things you value and need. Completing the exercise generates the feelings, frustrations, and emotions associated with making difficult decisions. By experiencing those feelings, you are more likely to recall the lesson in the future. Equally true, the story is visual—can't you see the paint chips scattering on the floor as they fall to their fate? That strong imagery component will make it easier for you to retell the story to a peer or member of your team after you set the book aside. Properly structured exercises can generate physical connections to content. Well-crafted stories can generate mental postcards of content. *Both play a role in shifting mindsets and changing behavior.* How does your list of reasons, above, compare to mine?

> Well-structured exercises can generate physical connections to content. Well-crafted stories can generate mental postcards of content.

Now, back to Riley and John. Let's reconsider Riley's meeting with John. In the activity, you only had space for a progressively smaller number of values. In my story, I only had space enough in the family room to select one color to paint the walls. In a time-constrained training program, John and Riley will only have space for limited content too. Based on your experience with the values activity and my paint-chip example, consider what Riley could have done differently to achieve better results with John.

Before reading further, jot down your ideas.

Two Powerful Questions to Determine Essential Content

Without a doubt, distilling content down to its most essential and vital elements requires work and discernment. Two powerful questions are at the heart of the distillation process. And while they can't make the process effortless, they can make it more manageable and improve your skills and effectiveness. Use these two questions to determine what content is essential:

- Question 1: What does success look like?
- Question 2: Does this get us closer to success? How?

These guiding questions will keep the process focused for you. They remove subjectivity and make tough decisions easier because they replace negotiating content arm-wrestle-style with selectively choosing content based on criteria—criteria set by your project sponsor!

Question 1: Starting at the Beginning

The parallel of Riley's meeting to the activity on the preceding pages is that the values you sorted through represent the training topics Riley presented to John. On their face, they all sound good. The question isn't if they are relevant, desirable, or valuable. The question is if they are *vital.* More specifically, are they vital to getting to the desired outcome? Let's be clear here: Training isn't actually about learning—it's about changing behavior and improving performance. Riley—and you—need to stop asking about *topics* and start talking about *skills.* Will these skills support learners in performing in the way and at the level that John requires? In other words, will these skills move the supervisors toward John's definition of success?

> Training isn't actually about learning—it is about changing behavior and improving performance.

From this perspective, Riley's starting point with John should not have been: "Which of these topics do we need to include?" Nor should it have been: "Which of these skills do the participants need to demonstrate?" It should have been: "What does success look like?", which is the first powerful distilling question.

Variations on this key question that Riley could use include:

- "What would you like to see happening after this training that isn't happening now?"
- "What should participants be able to do as a result of completing the training?"
- "If I observed a supervisor performing to your expectations after the training, what would I see?"
- "So that we can measure the effectiveness of the solution we develop, in one sentence, what would you say is the goal of this training?"
- "Of all the skills a supervisor should possess, which are most critical to his or her success?"
- "What are the two things supervisors are doing or not doing today that create the greatest number of undesired situations for you or for the organization?"
- "What metrics will the supervisors be held accountable for achieving?"
- "What are the criteria supervisors will be evaluated against in their performance evaluations?"

Many, if not all, of these questions will require follow-up—to probe, to clarify, and to add specificity. The follow-up questions will depend on the answers that are provided to the initial questions asked. In my experience, the initial responses to these questions are generally neither observable nor measurable—and you need them to be both. For example, if when asked "in one sentence, what would you say is the goal of this training?" John responded to Riley with, "the goal is for supervisors to be leading teams effectively," Riley would be no closer to knowing what his expectations are. Here are examples of some follow-up probing questions Riley could use in response:

- "OK, leading by using which skills exactly?"
- "Thank you for that. And what differentiates an effective supervisor from an ineffective one?"
- "Will you tell me three specific things the supervisors would need to do to rise to that statement?"

- "And what is the one behavior that is most critical to them meeting that goal? And the second most critical behavior?"

What vague goal statements have you been given in your projects? What follow-up questions will you ask to arrive at observable and measurable goals?

Question 2: Selecting the Vital Few

Once the end goal has been determined (or, in "instructional design speak," once the business outcomes have been identified), Riley can review her list of supervisory functions, skills, and topics with John and repeatedly pose the second question: "How does this content support the desired outcome?" (But she might be well advised to flip the content that doesn't make the cut over her shoulder a bit less dramatically than my paint chips met their fate.)

The distillation process that comes with this second question is critical. To avoid sounding flippant or interrogational, try using phrases such as:

- "Does this bring us closer to success? How?"
- "Can you tell me how this supports your goal?"
- "What, specifically, will the participants be required to do with this knowledge when performing their jobs?"
- "What is the direct line connection between this content and employees' performance requirements?"

To support you in using the two-question approach, Chapter 10 includes a job aid that pulls together variations on the two key questions introduced in this chapter.

Final Thoughts

When you approach the task of determining what to cut and what to include from the perspective of "what topics need to be addressed," you are setting yourself—and the learners—up for a rough ride. Instead, work to determine—in measurable, observable terms—the actions learners will be required to demonstrate on the job, and then confirm with the project sponsor that your understanding of what success looks like matches his. With that agreement established, collaborate to scrutinize each potential content piece to determine if it will move learners closer toward the goal or serve as a distraction.

Put It Into Practice

Review a recently completed course design and answer the following questions in relation to it:

1. Can you write a single statement that defines "success" for this course? Yes / No
   - If yes, what was it?
   - If no, where in the process did you miss your opportunity to identify it?
2. What content, in hindsight, was nonessential?
3. What valuable content, in hindsight, did not rise to being vital?
4. What vital content was included, and did it deserve greater attention in your design? (See Chapters 5, 6, and 7 for ideas.)
5. What vital content was left out?

Chapter Actions

- ❑ Determine what actions you will take based on your answers to the Put It Into Practice activity.
- ❑ Restructure your agenda template for project kick-off meetings to emphasize determining what success looks like and requiring content to rise to the standard of moving the learner closer to that success.
- ❑ Discuss with your training team how the two key questions will be used to identify essential content for all learning projects.
- ❑ Revisit your chapter-by-chapter action plan in Chapter 10 and update it with actions related to the content of this chapter.

5

Is Pre-Work a Magic Bullet?

50+ Strategies to Make Pre-Training Time Work

For the next three chapters, shift your mindset. Change the definition of your role from "creating a learning event" to that of "building a development continuum." When you do, you will be able to enhance learning outcomes and regain lost training time. Building a development continuum requires designing a complete learning solution—one that prepares learners for the core course, provides multiple touchpoints to the body of content, integrates on-the-job application, provides support to learners after the core event, and taps into the frequently overlooked role played by learners' managers. The strategies in Chapters 5, 6, and 7, respectively, will help you design a complete learning solution *before, during,* and *after* your time-constrained programs—and those that aren't severely time-constrained too.

Reclaiming time on either side of the core learning event doesn't mean loading up learners with volumes of pre-reading. Nor does it mean sending them away from training events with binders of "additional resources" to wade through independently. Rather, reclaiming time is about generating awareness of, expectations for, excitement over, and learning strategies for the core event long before participants log on or walk into the training room (addressed in this chapter). It is also about capitalizing on the time available in the core event (Chapter 6) and then creating follow-through, accountability, continued content exposure, and extended learning moments that connect back to the core event and the pre-event actions (Chapter 7).

Why Bother?

Does this sound like a lot of work? Work that you don't have time for, when you barely have time to create the event itself? Well, it will be work—but work that is worth the effort. This is one of the reasons Chapters 1 and 2 addressed the value of negotiating more time to create the learning solution.

Rest assured, your efforts to design a complete learning solution, starting with the pre-training time, will benefit learners, trainers, project sponsors, the business, and you too. Here's how:

- Learners will arrive enthused, prepared, informed, and with personal goals instead of mystified.
- Trainers can capitalize on having prepared learners, which positions them to use course time for enhanced skill development instead of level setting, cheerleading, and generating learners' internal motivation from a cold start.
- Your project sponsor and the business will realize greater returns from events characterized by participants who arrive with learning plans and trainers who can focus on supporting the attainment of those plans.
- And you—you will benefit from the Virtuous Cycle instead of the Vicious Cycle. The Vicious Cycle, outlined in Chapter 2, is the downward spiral created when ineffective training leads to less time for training, which results in less effective training, and so on. The Virtuous Cycle rotates upward (and is the goal you are working toward in Chapter 2). In the Virtuous Cycle, your successful learning solutions associate you with positive results, which garners respect for your skills and knowledge, which results in stakeholders seeking your input, listening to your ideas, and following your recommendations—which ultimately leads to even better results.

Exponential Value

The pre-training strategies in this chapter complement one another. The more you integrate, the more powerful their effect will be. They are grouped so we can talk about them more easily, but you will certainly see overlapping elements among the categories. As you work through the chapter, make note of specific ways you will incorporate the more than 50 ideas into your current program plans. Here is an overview of the categories of strategies in this chapter:

- Embrace tiny training.
- Educate learners' managers (or supervisors).
- Build manager support tools.
- Create a communication campaign.
- Entice and excite learners.
- Integrate pre-work.

(Note: There is an assessment in Chapter 10 you can use to rate yourself on how well are you reclaiming pre-training time.)

Embrace Tiny Training

Last year, while revising a pre-supervisory skills program, I was sourcing slide graphics. For one visual, related to ethical decision making, I envisioned a person grappling with a decision and all of his options hovering around him. That wasn't an easy image to locate. Then it hit me—create my own. So, I purchased a photo of a man faced with indecision and surrounded him with words in text boxes, but the words looked scattered. I decided to put them into circles, but the circles appeared flat and—frankly—boring. Spheres were the answer, I decided. Now my challenge was that I had no idea how to create a sphere in two dimensions that appeared three-dimensional. In need of my own learning event, I turned to the Internet, where I found an instructional video for creating a sphere in my software. After a few minutes of view a bit, click here and there, view a bit more, click a few more places, I had my sphere. Yay! Only mine wasn't quite as convincing as the finished sample in the instructional video—*that* sphere hovered over a shadow. To create a sphere *with* a shadow, I had to follow along with two separate videos: one for the sphere and another for the shadow. These instructional videos are examples of what I refer to as *tiny training.*

When you are facing the crunch of a shorter learning event, look at your list of essential content (from Chapter 4) and decide which elements must be included in the core course and which can become tiny training elements that precede or follow the core event. Mine your "nonessential content" for ideas of components that could be turned into games or tiny training elements that can be self-paced and optionally accessible. This is not the same as handing over dumps of resources to read. Not everyone will access the optional elements, but some will, especially if you make them engaging, interesting, challenging, relevant, fun, and reinforcing.

It may not even be necessary for you to create all of your tiny training elements yourself—you may be able to source existing resources. Look to your organization's learning subscription services (such as Lynda.com or Skillsoft's Skillport), search video content on YouTube or TED.com, and see what online courses available through providers such as Khan Academy and Coursera may complement your core course.

Here are a few examples of tiny training to get you thinking:

- For a class I designed on trust in the workplace, participants receive a link to a short, preexisting e-learning course on using interpersonal communication to build trust. At their option, they can access the resource before or after attending the ILT portion. The skills addressed in it are not covered in the core course, but they have a strong correlation to it. After the core course, the trainer emails a link for an online assessment instrument that measures the extent to which trust-building behaviors are being demonstrated and provides feedback on actions to improve trust levels, relationship by relationship. This is also optional—and motivated learners who value the core course do access it.
- For sales training, consider letting the learners develop some of the tiny training themselves. Set up an online area for participants to post 60-second videos of them delivering their best sales pitch, recorded on their smartphones. Set a course prerequisite to include posting a video, viewing the others, and bringing three best practices observed in them to class. After the core course, create a competition in which new videos are recorded and posted with their best post-training sales pitches. Make viewing the post-training videos and voting on the best one a course requirement too.

Educate Learners' Managers

Here is a secret—well, it isn't a secret, it just behaves like one—a manager's actions before an employee attends training has the single greatest impact on whether or not learning will transfer to the job. Read that again. The manager? Yes.

Keeping that in mind, consider these questions. Do participants at your organization arrive at training conflicted with choosing to engage in the learning or manage a workplace crisis from their smartphone? Are your learners more interested in whether they receive a certificate or credit hours than they are in developing their skills and applying them at work? Are blank stares provided in response to "What are you looking to get out of this session?" because zero forethought was given to the question? Do course evaluations include comments such as "I didn't know what to expect—but this was good"? If you said yes to any of these questions, here is the manager–learning success connection: What managers do or, more accurately, don't do before their employees attend training leads to these frustrating situations.

> **Try This**
>
> Tiny training is also a powerful technique for making training accessible to employees when and where they have time to focus on it, or when they *need* to access it. For example, if your organization's workforce is mobile, are you leveraging podcasts that can be downloaded and listened to during flights or on long commutes? If there are skills employees perform infrequently but must be performed correctly, how can you make guided instruction (such as my lessons in creating spheres and shadows) available to them? And, if your organization embraces and rewards collaborative effort, are you harnessing the potential of tools such as Padlet, Hootboard, Trello, Stoodle, or others? Aim to make your tiny training modular and nonsequential for greatest flexibility and user-perceived value.

You will want to take a two-pronged approach to educating the managers (or supervisors) of your learners. The first approach focuses on orienting managers to their role in training's success: establishing the critical influence their pre-training behaviors have on learners' ability to succeed, providing tools to support them in that role, and encouraging them to take actions that will lead to increased success. The second approach is orienting managers to the content in the course by developing tools to brief them on what is covered in the program. Sometimes, managers may even need to learn the content themselves so they can better support their learners back at their jobs.

Orienting Managers to Their Role

To help managers embrace their critical role in their employees' development success, you will need to decide how to communicate to managers the three most influential factors in employees learning new skills and successfully transferring them to improved job performance:

1. What the employees' *managers* do before the training
2. What the *trainer* does during the training (addressed in Chapter 6)
3. What the employees' *managers* do after the training (addressed in Chapter 7)

Successful training requires a manager sandwich! These findings are based on the research of Broad and Newstrom (1992) published in their book *Transfer of Training*—a great read. It is the learning function's responsibility to educate managers on the undeniable influence their actions or inactivity have on learners' success or failure. So, what sorts of things can a manager do as a pre-training partner in the learning process? Consider this list:

- Convey a sense of excitement for the learning opportunity.
- Inform employees of what to expect from the program.
- Establish expectations for each employee—founded in actionable behaviors expected upon returning from training.
- Build pre-training learning strategies with each employee (list questions to obtain answers to, select a project or challenge to bring to training as a personal case study, set a plan for note-taking and action planning, determine how they will contribute to the course, and so on).
- Manage employees' workloads and assignments so they are able to focus fully on the learning opportunity.

Without your help, a manager will be hard pressed to effectively do any but the final item on the list. Chances are that you are already doing some of the things listed in this section. That's great. As you read, question how you can do those more effectively, and note those you are not doing—and what you will do to change that.

The following are actions you can take that will enhance a manager's pre-training effectiveness as a partner to the learning process:

- Write engaging course descriptions (this idea is expanded on later in the chapter).
- Provide guidance on who should attend your course—and who should not.
- Collaborate with business units on course scheduling so that staff participates in professional development activities together.
- Make direct requests of managers to schedule employee training time as a continuum to include: 1) allocating pre-training time to set learning goals, bring closure to open projects, complete pre-requisite actions, set an out-of-office notification, and so on; and 2) allocating post-training time to implement action plans, brief their manager on the experience, reenter their role, apply new behaviors (which may require more time initially), share learning with other employees, and so on.
- Protect learning time by asking managers to insulate employees from interruptions during training. Examples include reassigning their core responsibilities temporarily and not texting/calling/emailing employees during the learning event.
- Coordinate with managers prior to the training to build after-training actions into performance standards for job functions.

Orienting Managers to the Content

Not included in the preceding list are strategies to enhance managers' awareness of program content—the second prong in educating learners' managers. This category warrants its own list. It is challenging, at best, for managers or supervisors to support an employee in applying new skills and course content when the skills and content are unknown to them. And—if you are being honest—there is probably a lot of room for improvement in what you are currently doing in this area.

How much managers need to know—and the best way for them to learn it—will vary based on many organizational, scheduling, and course-specific factors. Here are a number of different ways to raise managers' awareness and skills. Choose the most ambitious option your project constraints will allow:

- Develop an abbreviated version of the program for managers to attend. This is not a briefing, presentation, or lip service to training. It should be a compact learning event that introduces the same skills, develops them in the managers, and provides tools you created to assist managers in supporting staff with the skills following training. Schedule the delivery of this event in advance of the employee version.
- Weigh the advantages and disadvantages of allowing managers to join the employees' sessions. If you opt for this, require managers to participate—not just observe—and advise trainers to ensure that managers are not grouped in task teams with their direct reports.
- Provide managers with a complete set of participant materials and a roadmap highlighting critical content, concepts, tools, and resources.
- Develop a one-page course summary tool for managers to reference while setting training expectations with employees and supporting them post-training.
- Provide managers with the course agenda. Include the learning objectives and connect the objectives with the employees' on-the-job performance expectations.

Build Manager Support Tools

When you are drafting your proposal or project deliverables, extend your development plans beyond creating participant and facilitator materials to include manager materials too. In addition to the resources you create to orient them to the course content, discussed in the preceding section, think about what tools you can provide to make managers more effective at setting expectations for the training with employees before they attend. Here are some ideas to consider:

- Scripted language for pre-training conversations with staff.
- Templates of training contracts to complete and commit to with their staff. Be sure to include space for the specific actions both parties will be responsible for and deadlines for performing them.
- Learning plan templates (see multiple ideas in Chapter 10).

- Prepared emails (discussed later in this chapter).
- An interview guide for the day after training, which could include coaching questions and course-specific content questions, as well as appropriate answers!

Create a Communication Campaign

You may have designed and developed an incredibly powerful course on negotiation skills, but if no one knows about it, how useful is it really? It is not enough to add the course title and description to the training calendar and wait for enrollments. You also need to manage its messaging. In effect, you need to market it.

Start by documenting a communication plan for the course, including campaign elements and scheduling:

> "Build it and they will come" is a chancy strategy. Instead, take your cues from marketing and advertising professionals, who have mastered the arts of building enthusiasm, generating hype, and creating value propositions that lead to engaged choices.

- **Throw a broad net.** Include messages from the participants' managers, the trainer, the administrative team, and the program's sponsor, influencers, or other key figures.
- **Factor in timing.** When will each element be experienced for maximum effect and who will coordinate the timing? Go a step further by factoring in such influences as peak work periods, holiday schedules, and preexisting events such as board meetings, industry conferences, national awareness days/weeks, and so on.
- **Plan for multiple communication channels.** Include emails (see ideas below), break room flyers, posters, newsletters, and internal website articles.
- **Share success stories from previous participants.** Go beyond "it was a great class" to workplace examples of results they achieved by using the skills developed and the tools provided in the program.

Next, create the elements. Ideally, they will build on one another, complement each other, repeat without being redundant, be engaging, and motivate learners. Here is a list to inspire your pre-training elements (see Chapter 7 for post-training elements of the communication campaign):

- **Shoot a short, engaging video of the champion or a key organizational figure.** Aim for a fun, "infotainment" flair that presents why this course is being provided, what learners can expect, and what managers will be expecting too.
- **Develop a conversation guide to facilitate manager/employee discussions prior to training.** This can include scripted language as well as recommended meeting outcomes. Guide managers to generate excitement for the development opportunity, share positive reasons the employee was selected to attend the program, identify benefits to the employee of attending, and set expectations of how the learning will be applied.
- **Ghost-write emails for trainers to send to participants prior to training.** Set a positive and collaborative tone for the event. Share the planned outcomes and intended benefits to the learners. Tell learners what to bring to participate fully. Explain and attach any prerequisite actions. (See a worksheet with tips and a sample trainer email in Chapter 10. See Chapter 7 for a list of post-event email ideas.)
- **Ghost-write emails for managers to send to participants prior to training.** Reinforce pre-training conversations by ghost-writing additional emails for managers to send to participants at designated intervals prior to training:
  - **One month prior:** This message should reiterate enthusiasm for the course, why the employee was selected, and benefits of attending to the employee and work unit, as well as share the course outline and learning objectives.
  - **Two weeks prior:** Draft this message to provide greater detail on course content and takeaways, share manager's expectations for participation during and application of learning after the event, and provide a training contract template to be completed and executed by the manager and learner.

  - **Two days prior:** This short message should remind the learner to set an out-of-office notice for when she will be in training, encourage her to enjoy the learning event, and schedule time to reconvene after the training to review her learning implementation plan.
- **Ghost-write emails for the administrative team or learning management system (LMS) to distribute.** Include course title and description, reminders of items learners should bring or download, and all logistical information.
  - **For synchronous e-learning,** include dates, time zone of start and end times, directions for accessing the event, and a contact for troubleshooting.
  - **For self-paced learning,** include deadlines for completing the coursework, links to content or directions for accessing it, and instructions to ensure they receive credit hours.
  - **For face-to-face instructor-led learning,** include dates, start and end times, address, parking instructions, whether meals will be provided, and so on.

Entice and Excite Learners

Think about your course as potential learners would. Take into account that they may be facing workplace challenges, may be both personally and professionally tapped out, or may not even be aware that they are scheduled to attend this course. How can you make the training appeal to learners? Try these ideas:

- Write course descriptions that describe how the program will solve a problem, save time, reduce expense, minimize waste, or otherwise benefit the *learner*—in a meaningful way. The emphasis on learner here is key. You won't excite learners by telling them how your program benefits the *organization*. You want them to see how training will help them personally perform better. (See Figure 5-1.)
- Provide examples of what participants will walk away with. These can be woven into your communication campaign elements (discussed earlier).

Figure 5-1. Course Description Reworked

Typical Course Description

The SimpleSolutions Software Skills class is a half-day event targeted to employees with agenda-item-writing responsibilities. The course will orient participants to the new interface and cover creating and revising agenda items. Participants will learn how to log in, write an agenda item, attach exhibits, forward items for approval, make changes, and submit items for inclusion on the commission meeting agenda. This is mandatory training for all administrative personnel as well as all employees involved in the writing of or approval of agency agenda items.

Rewritten With Marketing in Mind

Tired of the manual process for creating and revising agenda items? Exhausted by tracking down who is reviewing the item and how close it is to approval? You are not alone, but you will be one of the first to begin using the new SimpleSolutions software system to streamline this process. After this hands-on, practical training session, you will be able to use SimpleSolutions to create agenda items for the October 1, 20XX commission meeting. And we are going to set you up for success! The learning objectives, below, outline all of the skills you will walk away with.

Now You Try It

Rewrite a course description for a recent or upcoming course you are developing.

- Design succinct, story-telling infographics that summarize your course's key elements, data gathered from course evaluations, or examples of applied learning testimonials. Target the messaging in them to your intended audience—what managers care about and what learners will be motivated by are distinct.
- Create a learner-driven discussion area using social media, your LMS, or collaboration tools such as SharePoint, Yammer, Bitrix24, SocialCast, or Chatter, where you prompt discussions and then allow learners to drive their direction.
- Make evaluation data from previous deliveries public within the organization.

Integrate Pre-Work

Sure, pre-work is a tool that can be leveraged to extend the development continuum when training time is reduced. The Introduction of this book, however, calls out shifting the burden of a time-constrained training to learners with a "pre-work dump" as something *not* to do. There is a simple reason for this: Most pre-work isn't work at all—it is reading. A lot of reading. And there is an inherent problem with that—in any given group of learners, some will read it and some won't. That begs this question: "Is the pre-reading content essential to the core course?" If it is and some have not read it, then what is a trainer to do? If it isn't and others took work hours or personal time to read it before attending, they will ask "why did I bother?"

So, pre-*reading* is not the key to your success at managing the reduced training time challenge. Pre-*work*, however, can be part of a bigger solution—as long as it is done well. If you choose to assign pre-work, here are a few best practices that will make it beneficial rather than a burden:

- Give credit hours for the time required to complete the pre-work.
- Explain the connection of the pre-work to the training and specify if it must be completed prior to attending or not.
- Inform the learners' managers of the pre-work requirements.
- Provide ample advance notice of the pre-work assignment and an estimate of the time required to complete it.
- Provide clear instructions for completing the pre-work.

- Request that learners acknowledge receipt of the pre-work, and follow up with those who do not reply to ensure it was received and the expectation is clear.
- When you must provide baseline data (that is, reading) to level-set a group of learners, be clear on the expectations. Explain the level-setting purpose of the material, disclose whether it will be actively used, referenced in passing, or not explicitly covered in the session, and offer guidance on how to tackle it. For example, skim sections to refresh existing knowledge, read sections that are new or unfamiliar, and bring questions on content as needed.

And, here are a few activity ideas for engaging pre-work for learners:

- Completing pre-assessments that would otherwise be done during training, which allows learners to work at their own pace without peer pressure.
- Conducting research in support of real-world case studies. For example, for an advanced negotiations skills course, in which participants role play vendor negotiations based on actual prior events, the pre-work included four hours to prepare for the in-training activity. Learners were directed to learn as much as they could about the vendor, its officers, their business practices, previous contracts with the organization, and so on and then prepare their negotiation worksheets (based on tools introduced in the 101-level negotiation skills prerequisite).
- Researching best practices associated with the training topic and bringing findings to training.
- Reading *brief* background content aligned with a set of questions to be discussed in training.
- Completing self-assessment exercises that provide insight to a learner's style, strengths, attitudes, and so on related to the training topic.
- Recording questions, a current challenge, or a pain point that learners will come to training looking for answers to, strategies for, or tools to relieve.
- Accessing a tiny training component (discussed previously) that you may have created or sourced.

Final Thoughts

You are putting learners at a distinct disadvantage when you expect them to arrive at a learning event—face-to-face or online—and go from unaware and potentially uninterested to engaged and productive in mere minutes. Chances are good that you allow your car more time to prepare for highway speeds than many course designs provide for learners to go from zero to 90 mph.

It isn't just about what learners do before the event. In fact, it is mostly about what their *managers* do before it—and as a corollary, what *you* do to position managers to succeed at what is required of them.

If there is a magical training-effectiveness unicorn out there to be discovered, it lives in the realm of pre-training time. Tap into the powerful influence this time can be with as many pre-training strategies as you can manage.

Put It Into Practice

Divide this circle into a pie chart of three sections. Each piece should represent the percentage of time and effort you devote to designing and developing resources, support, activities, and so on for: *pre-training, training,* and *post-training.*

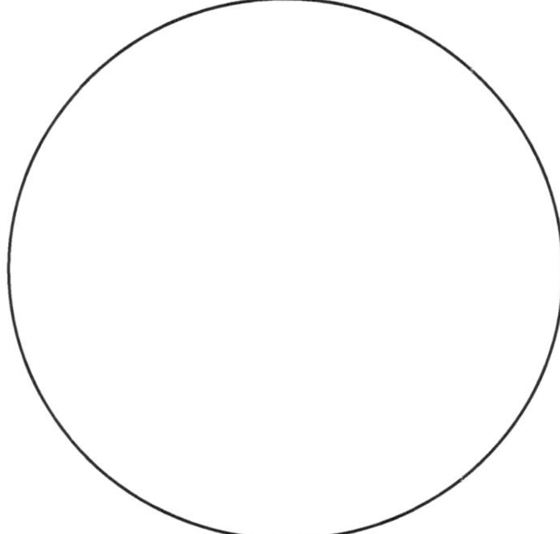

Considering your pie chart, above, how would you describe the proportion of time you dedicate to developing *pre-training* tools?

It is too small | It is just right | It is too large

What actions will you take to adjust the time and effort dedicated to developing pre-training resources?

1.

2.

3.

Place checkmarks beside the strategies you will begin to leverage or expand the role of in your pre-training deliverables. For any you check, record notes on your plan to integrate them.

- ❑ Embrace tiny training.
  Notes:

- ❑ Educate learners' managers (or supervisors).
  Notes:

- ❑ Build manager support tools.
  Notes:

- ❑ Create a communication campaign.
  Notes:

- ❑ Entice and excite learners.
  Notes:

- ❑ Integrate pre-work.
  Notes:

Chapter Actions

- ❑ Self-assess how well you are reclaiming pre-training time using the assessment instrument in Chapter 10.
- ❑ Start thinking small—look for opportunities to source, build, integrate, and leverage tiny training elements.
- ❑ Read *Transfer of Training* (Broad & Newstrom 1992). (This may seem to be an ironic suggestion after our discussion in this chapter about reading, but it is vital content for designers and trainers alike. It will give you the broad underpinnings of transfer of learning concepts needed to create better training in a time crunch.)
- ❑ Add support tools for managers to your proposed deliverables, allocate time to create them, and orient managers to them.
- ❑ Think big—extend your development role to include creating items that will not be experienced by learners during the learning event but are part of your overall development continuum.
- ❑ Draft a communication campaign plan for the current program you are working on, or consider what you should have built into one for your last course if you are currently between projects.
- ❑ Pay attention to marketing and advertising campaigns that grab your attention and influence your actions, and then consider how you can leverage those same kinds of strategies for your courses and their target participants.
- ❑ Commit to replacing pre-reading with pre-work.
- ❑ Revisit your chapter-by-chapter action plan in Chapter 10 and update it with actions related to the content of this chapter.

6

What Strategies Make Limited Training Time Meaningful?

65 Techniques That Lead to Better Training

In the last chapter, we began to explore the idea of building a development continuum with ways to effectively reclaim time *before* the training event. In this chapter, we turn to ways to make the most of the limited time *during* the training.

So, which learning strategies provide the greatest return with limited training time? Those that engage learners and those that allow for personal reflection. Those that cause learners to work hard and those that let learners play with purpose. Those that let learners fail in a safe setting and those that set learners up for success. These are not conflicting opposites. They are the mix of learning strategies that provide the greatest return in a limited amount of time—and, frankly, in any amount of time.

Your challenge when course time is tight will be remaining true to these tenets. This chapter provides a suite of four tactics to get you there and more than 65 examples of and ideas for applying them. The techniques complement one another and, when combined, become exponentially more valuable at increasing retention and performance when training time has been cut. Resist the urge to think of these strategies as standalone. Instead, look for ways to leverage all four into your final solutions—regardless of delivery format.

The techniques addressed in this chapter apply equally to instructor-led, self-paced e-learning, online synchronous, and one-on-one training events:

- ✓ Shift from information provider to information miner.
- ✓ Be a curator—not a librarian.
- ✓ Integrate six essential components to maximize learning.
- ✓ Leverage the trainer's function.

(Note: See Chapter 10 for an assessment you can use to rate yourself on how well you are maximizing your training time.)

Shift From Information Provider to Information Miner

The single greatest strategy to make the most of limited training time is for you to redefine your role. You need to make the shift from information *provider* to information *miner.* A provider gives information to learners, whereas a miner helps them discover or "mine" it themselves. How can you know if you are a provider or a miner? You will want to make this fundamental shift if any of the following are true:

> **Insider Tip**
> No time to read this chapter? Here is a key takeaway: Just about *any* activity that is instructionally sound and isn't lecture will have greater return than merely talking to participants.

- ❑ After or during a course, learners say "Why didn't you just send me the slides? I could have read it myself without coming here."
- ❑ This is your learners' e-learning experience: Read a slide, click "next," answer a question based on the previous slide's content, click "next," repeat, and so on and so on.
- ❑ The design of your instructor-led program centers around a steady stream of expert practitioners arriving to share their knowledge, experiences, and best practices with participants, followed by Q&A sessions—to "make it interactive."

- ❑ The majority of your design and development time is spent re-packaging existing information into new delivery channels, such as manuals, reference guides, job aids, videos, infographics, files to be posted on a shared drive, or articles you will post to the course's blog *instead* of designing activities that require interaction with the content.
- ❑ After leading a full-day course, you are exhausted and your voice is strained from lecturing—endlessly.
- ❑ In your synchronous web-based programs, learners attending live sessions have the same experience as those listening to the recorded version of the session.
- ❑ As a manager, you are providing the training team with tomes of information and setting the expectation that participants "need all of this."

> **Make the Shift from Information Provider to Information Miner**
>
> When you look at your role through this new lens, when you go from pushing content onto people to pulling it from them, you increase the value of the learning and lessen the time required to achieve meaningful learning.
>
> It certainly may be true that you can say it, share it, hand out a job aid with it, or demonstrate it in less time than it takes to draw the information out. But saying or sharing it is not the same as *learning* it.

Compare the preceding list of classic training faux pas with this list of learning strategies that provide the greatest return in limited time:

- ✓ Those that engage.
- ✓ Those that allow for personal reflection.
- ✓ Those that cause learners to work hard.
- ✓ Those that let learners play, with purpose.
- ✓ Those that let learners fail in a safe setting.
- ✓ Those that set learners up for success.

It seems so obvious here. Dumping data on people—whether through lecture, video, slide content, or other means—is not conducive to learning. Instead, honor the learners' existing knowledge, draw on their experiences, bring their context into the learning event, challenge them, support them, provide resources, and let them have fun—that is what causes real magic to happen.

How to Make the Shift

Your challenge as an instructional designer is not finding the most compelling, clear, and straightforward way to *explain* a technique, model, action, or piece of knowledge. Instead, having found the most direct route, your challenge is devising a process that, when followed, will consistently cause learners to discover it for themselves.

To give you an example of what I mean, I will use the strategy to explain the strategy. If this chapter were a learning event in which I wanted to mine information instead of provide it, I might follow this approach (detailed first for an instructor-led course and then for a self-paced e-learning program):

Facilitator Guide Excerpt

Display Slide: Which learning strategies provide the greatest return in limited training time?

Say: You already know the answer to this question.

Introduce Activity: Think of a training you attended that was awful. Write down three to five reasons it was ineffective for you. Then share your ideas with a partner and find commonalities.

Continue Activity: Now, how about a learning event you experienced that you valued and was beneficial to you? Let's call it effective training. What made it so? Again, write three to five specific reasons why, share your answers with a partner, and find the commonalities.

Debrief: Chart answers to both questions on separate charts using the round-robin technique.

Say: (referring to the first chart) There you go! That is a good list of what *not* to do when you shorten training time.

Continue Debrief: As needed, supplement discussion with other items that belong on the Awful list, such as:

- ✘ There was no relevance to my job.
- ✘ The curriculum insulted my intelligence.
- ✘ It wasn't clear what I was supposed to get from the course.
- ✘ I had to fight to stay awake.
- ✘ The few activities included provided no challenge for me.
- ✘ I received no feedback on my performance during the exercises.
- ✘ I was overwhelmed by the amount of information just being pushed at me.
- ✘ There was nothing in the design to support me doing anything differently on the job after the training.

Continue Debrief: Discuss how to achieve the effective training strategies listed on the second chart. As needed, supplement discussion with other items that belong on the Effective list, such as:

- ✓ It solved a problem I was facing (or provided practice with tools to solve it).
- ✓ It was specific to my position.
- ✓ I was challenged to bring my knowledge into the course and share it with others.
- ✓ I learned from my peers as much as from the course itself.
- ✓ Activities were structured to expose information as I worked through them.
- ✓ I received feedback in the moment in such a way that even when I had an incorrect answer the reasoning was made clear to me.

Say: These effective training characteristics are foundational to any good training design. You will want to—I'll go further—you will *need* to maintain these traits in your shorter learning events if you intend to deliver better training in half the time.

And for a self-paced e-learning, I'd follow the same logic for the exercise above in five screens, as shown in basic mock-ups below.

Screen 1:

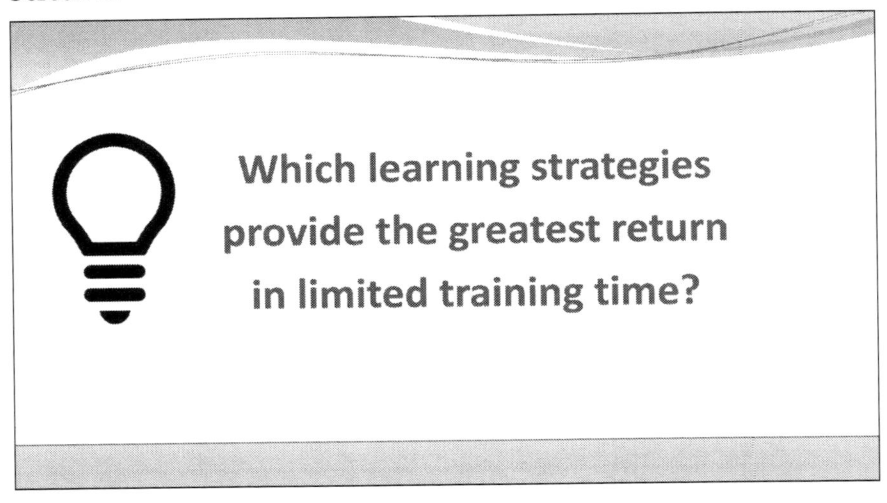

Which learning strategies provide the greatest return in limited training time?

Screen 2:

Exercise:

Think of an awful training you attended. Write three to five reasons it was ineffective.

Next...recall a learning event you valued. What made it beneficial to you? Record your answers.

Compare your ideas to these examples...

Animation on Screen 2 when "next" is clicked: Arrow pointing to left screen area with text "Avoid these." Arrow pointing to right screen area with text "Integrate these."

Screen 3:

Awful Training

- There was no relevance to my job
- The curriculum insulted my intelligence
- It wasn't clear what I was supposed to get from the course
- I had to fight to stay awake
- The few activities that were included provided no challenge for me
- I received no feedback on my performance during the exercises
- I was overwhelmed by the amount of information just being pushed at me
- There was nothing in the design to support me doing anything differently on the job after the training

Effective Training

- It solved a problem I was facing / provided practice with tools to solve it
- It was specific to my position
- I was challenged to bring my knowledge into the course and share it with others
- I learned from my peers as much as from the course itself
- Activities were structured to expose information as I worked through them
- I received feedback in the moment in such a way that even when I had an incorrect answer the reasoning was made clear to me

Screen 4: Dissolve heading and left screen content on Screen 3. Replace with heading and left screen content below.

How will you create effective, shorter training?

These characteristics are foundational to any good training design!

You will want to – in fact, need to – maintain these traits in your shorter learning events if you intend to deliver better training in half the time

Effective Training

- It solved a problem I was facing / provided practice with tools to solve it
- It was specific to my position
- I was challenged to bring my knowledge into the course and share it with others
- I learned from my peers as much as from the course itself
- Activities were structured to expose information as I worked through them
- I received feedback in the moment in such a way that even when I had an incorrect answer the reasoning was made clear to me

Screen 5:

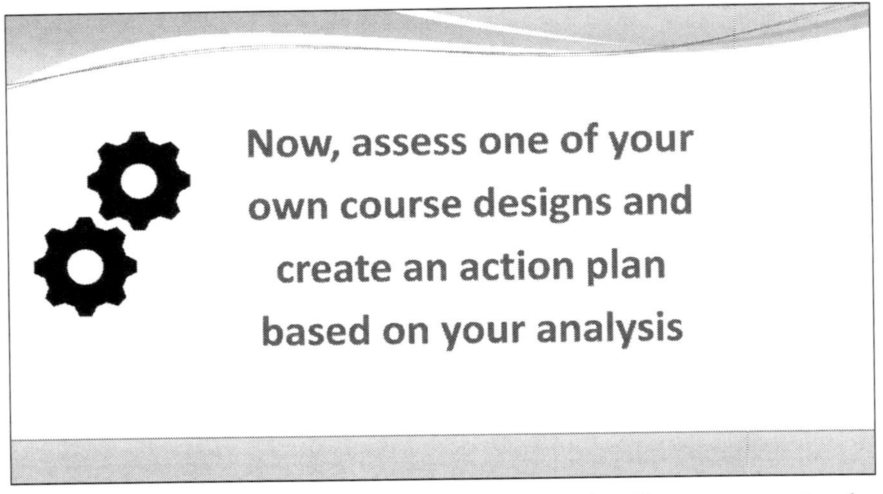

Do you see information mining in these examples? Do you recognize the subtle shift from telling to asking? From listening (on the participant's part) to learning? Did you notice the examples begin by drawing out what learners already know and then supplement, add to, or redirect as needed—based on where the learners are coming from? When you hold "prepared content" to present as an after-action review, as an answer guide, as supplemental facilitator content, and so on, you are making the shift to mining.

I have heard it said that attorneys never ask a question of witnesses and defendants on the stand to which they don't already know the answer. Attorneys use questions to tell a story, to mine for information they want the jury to hear and remember. You can use the same approach to mine for information you want learners to remember and draw upon as they perform their jobs.

Beyond the Socratic Approach

Questions are a sure-fire way to mine for information, but they are not the only way. Exercises that require participants to explore, make comparisons, draw conclusions, solve problems, find connections, and apply models also "mine." In short, let people use their knowledge during class. Adult learners always know something—it might not be the "right something"—but they know it! And when you draw out what they know, your learning event can validate it, meet and redirect it, inform it, or correct it as needed. Here are two examples of mining for information that are not based on asking questions:

- In a grammar course, instead of providing definitions of the parts of speech, prepare sets of cards to be distributed to small groups. Half of the cards list a part of speech and the remaining cards define the parts of speech. Groups will match the cards as best they can. In my experience, once noun and verb get paired off quickly and correctly, people begin singing songs about conjunctions and match it, then the debates begin over adverb and adjective. The result is that learners quickly assess what they have and don't have mastery of, they learn from one another, and they become receptive to receiving instruction. (For an online course, convert this to a drag-and-drop matching activity.)
- For a managerial e-learning program focused on addressing declining employee performance, forgo screens outlining steps to take and instead create a branched scenario that allows learners to choose actions and follow them through their natural progression—like a build-your-own-adventure book. If the manager's chosen path leads to an undesired outcome, she can go back and make new choices, request guidance prompts as she re-navigates the scenario, or opt to receive feedback on the choices she made. Try using Twine (at twinery.org) to build your branched scenarios. (For an instructor-led course, convert this to an out-of-seat learning partner activity. Provide pairs with a scenario card and, based on the action they choose to take, direct them to a station in the room where they find the result of their choice and their next step options, and so on.)

Be a Curator—Not a Librarian

Librarians are great! They know so much. Even better, they know how to find out what they currently know little or nothing about. They are amazing professionals. But don't model your instructional design style on library science.

Instead, think about a curator. Art curators oversee every detail of an exhibition. They select content for presentation. They stage their selections in ways that create interest. A curator's job is similar to a movie director's in that they both oversee every detail of the production and are selective regarding what to include and ruthless at cutting away excess.

The word *curator* comes from the Latin *curare*, meaning "to take care." As an instructional designer, your role is to take care of the learners—providing what they require to succeed and insulating and protecting them from, well, everything else.

There is an odd temptation in shortened learning events to take out the very parts that cause learning to happen. Avoid that urge. Exercises take time. Exploration takes time. Making new connections takes time. And time is limited in your shorter learning events. You really have two choices: Eliminate the actions that cause learning to happen (please don't make that choice) or eliminate the content that Chapter 4 helped you determine is not essential.

So, put up a fence. Limit admission. And curate an exceptional experience. Here are some strategies to try:

- If you are jumping around in this book and skipped Chapter 4, its two-question technique is designed to help you distinguish vital content from valuable material so that you can curtail the volume of material included in your course—instead of the foundations of sound instructional design.
- You can also create multiple versions of courses and target them to specific population subsets. In this approach, you design the "base course" and tailor content based on the participants. For example:
  - Your global call center academy can be customized for teams working in the United States, Canada, Asia, and the European Union. Differing regulations, cultural norms, customer expectations, and product features are a few of the variables that may influence what is vital and what is nonessential in the multiple versions.
  - Your sales academy can have two tracks—one for inside sales and another for outside sales.

  - — For a supervisory skills program, design a field version and an office version.
  - — Your annual e-learning compliance training can have a track for managers/supervisors and another for staff.
- In multi-session courses, create smooth transitions from one session to the next. A curated event seems to flow effortlessly with each element positioned in relation to the others. Structure your courses with the same care and logic. Seek an objective perspective from someone outside the design process to ensure that the connections you think are there are evident to someone experiencing the course for the first time.
- Resist the urge to squeeze in more than you have time for.

Integrate Six Essential Components to Maximize Learning

When you are building your design—the process the course will follow—integrate and defend the inclusion of these six components:

1. Context
2. Introductions with intent
3. Goal setting
4. Application
5. Self-reflection
6. Call to action

These are not elements to include in addition to your essential content; *they are the framework that will carry the content.* Create the six components by building activities and exercises that integrate the essential content you identified, as shown in the examples that follow.

Context

Creating context will ground and orient the learners. Context establishes relevance, generates interest, enhances learners' internal motivation, connects the microcosm of the learning event to the macrocosm of the desired business outcome, and more. It provides learners with answers to the critical question stack of why this, why now?

Here are five ideas on how to create context:

- Share the history of why the course was developed and why the participants were selected to participate. Here is how *not* to do this: "In the past year, multiple harassment lawsuits have been brought against the organization. Therefore, all employees must complete this sensitivity training program as a mandatory requirement." Instead, consider something along these lines: "When the executive team was studying the factors that we need in place to attract the best talent and build a reputation as *the* firm to work for, 'a culture of respect and tolerance' was repeatedly mentioned in employee surveys and focus groups. As a result, . . . [be sure you maintain a positive focus when completing this and don't tack on the earlier "mandatory requirement" language]."
- Pose a challenge that is relatable to the learners and that the course will provide strategies to manage. Invite input on how they would react (even if rhetorically in self-paced e-learning), probe to determine how effective these approaches have been, and present the value of this course in that context. Will it make them more effective, more productive, less stressed, or something else?
- Open with a story that explains how the program content benefited you or a previous program participant and *connect that* to how the course will help the learner hearing the story.
- Record a short video vignette of program graduates sharing *specific* ways they have *used* course content. Think in terms of results—did they streamline a process, reduce rework caused by errors, solve a problem, close a deal, coach an employee through a behavior issue? Testimonials of this sort will create context in a way "I loved the class," "I wish I attended sooner," and "The program changed how I do my job" just won't.
- Show a graphic depicting the skills and behaviors required for promotion, to build a skill, or to attain a certification, and so on and indicate how this course aligns with those requirements.

Introductions With Intent

Do not forgo introductions—just skip the waste of time so many are. There is a camp of designers, trainers, and learners who enjoy the novelty and fun of opening activities that have no direct relationship to the goals of the workshop. But time is precious—learners expect that we won't waste theirs with silliness, pop culture, sports statistics, and so on when there is no connection to what they came to learn. When time to train is tight, any allowance for losing time on whimsy is lost.

Does that mean drop the fun? No! Fun introductions set a tone for the learning event and begin building a comfortable atmosphere for learners to be vulnerable together and help one another grow. It does mean that you should design introductions that *integrate content* though.

Ideally, introductions set a tone for the event, are informative and fun, *and* are directly connected to the goals of the workshop. Let's look at an example of a popular icebreaker, Two Truths and a Lie, and how it can be converted to an "Introduction with Intent." The activity typically involves each person telling the group three statements about themselves—one of which is not true—and the group guesses which is the lie. If a time management course is designed to open with this activity, while the group may have fun, 20 or 30 minutes of time management training will have been spent *not* managing time. Converted to integrate content, the activity might be scripted as shown in Figure 6-1 on the next page.

Insider Tip

If your courses are led by someone else, provide specific introduction activity instructions in the facilitator guide. Also consider if guidance prompts are needed in the visuals to ensure the introductions occur as you planned them.

As revised, the activity in Figure 6-1 serves multiple purposes:

- ✓ Allows learners to meet and get to know about one another.
- ✓ Surfaces strategies this group already uses.
- ✓ Promotes peer-to-peer content exchanges that upcoming instructor-to-learner content exchanges can supplement.
- ✓ Respects the knowledge, skills, and experience the learners bring.
- ✓ Helps the facilitator reinforce course material from the learners' context.
- ✓ Moves the group toward the goal of the session.
- ✓ Encourages having fun too!

FIGURE 6-1. TWO TRUTHS AND A LIE, RESCRIPTED

Say: Let's have some fun identifying what you are already doing well and generate a list of time management best practices at the same time. Please think of three effective time management strategies: two that you are consistently performing—your "truths"—and one that you should be doing but are not—your "lie."

Invite: Learners to share their name, position, and their three statements as others guess their lie.

Record: Group's truths on one chart and their lies on another chart during the activity.

Discuss:
- Reasons the lies are not being implemented consistently
- Benefits learners would derive from applying all of the strategies—truths and lies

Allow: Time for self-reflection on the lists and action planning/note taking.

Do: Refer to charts throughout the course and tailor delivery to this group based on chart content. Use them to reinforce course material from the participants' context.

Here are seven ideas for creating introductions with intent:

- Build a crossword puzzle of topic-related acronyms that although commonly used are not easily defined. Set activity rules that require learners to work on each clue with a new partner.
- Modify a standard "mingle and meet three new people" activity so that participants mingle and meet three topic-related best practices. Distribute name tags with the word "name" replaced with "idea." Direct participants to write their ideas instead of their names.
- In a change management course, plan an action that will create discomfort for most participants (require them to change seats, place their shoes on the wrong feet, write down three lines of information using their nondominant hand, or so on). Then ask them to reflect on how they felt, why, and how this forced

change may align with a change they are facing at work or in life. Read out a list of prepared common responses and have participants move to stations in the room associated with each (such as, I needed additional time, I resented being told what to do, I was less confident). Invite participants who have not moved to a station to share their unique responses and form a final group. Direct learners to meet the people at their station.

- Provide learners with a set of story starter cards. They can list phrases such as these examples: "there was a time when . . . ," "I'll never forget . . . ," "I learned an important lesson when . . . ," and others you create. Each participant draws a card, reads it aloud, and completes the story with information relevant to the session.
- Provide learners with a set of cards imprinted with common traffic signs (U-turn, no parking, one way, detour, lane ends, slippery ahead, and so on). Participants each draw a card and relate the sign on their cards to the session topic.
- Display a caricature of a person that emphasizes the head, heart, and hands. Tell learners to prepare a self-introduction that connects to what they think (head), how they feel (heart), and what they do well (hands) in relation to the training topic.
- Draw on your favorite icebreakers and infuse them with content.

Even self-paced programs should include introductions with intent. Although there aren't other participants to meet, the one learner should be introduced to and begin interacting with the content of the course. It may help you to think of this as a "warm up exercise" in a self-paced program. If you consistently design self-paced learning, reread the list above and look for modifications you can make to tailor them to a one-learner environment, such as rhetorical questions, independent activity, brainstorming, and so on.

Goal Setting

Some participants are eager learners. Some are not. Some have researched a course and enrolled in it because of the potential benefit they anticipate deriving from the experience. Others are reluctantly enrolled in a course and directed by their manager to "show up" at a certain time and place—with no more interest in the event than wondering if there will be doughnuts and if those doughnuts will have sprinkles.

Building goal setting into your course designs will benefit both groups. In instructor-led training, it will also benefit the facilitator. Here is how easily you can do it. After establishing the course context and leading learners into a "soft-touch" of the content with an introductions with intent activity, share the learning objectives, invite learners to review them, and then ask the learners to set a personal goal for the session.

These actions are not random but intentional. Whether self-motivated or not, upon entering a learning event all learners will be in a better position to establish a personal goal for the session once they know more about its planned direction. You can compare this to taking a family road trip. Before seeking input on each family member's goals for the trip, giving them a sense of the car's final destination informs their choices and greatly increases your ability to deliver on their goals.

Here are six ways to invite learners to set their learning goals. Tailor these ideas to your needs, or create your own:

- **Display a slide, screen, or flip chart that says:** "Complete this sentence: This program will be beneficial to me if ______________________________."
- **Ask:** "What is a challenge you are dealing with today that relates to our topic? Grab an index card and write it down. You can share it with me or hold onto it—up to you." (Note: In e-learning, this can be done rhetorically. In synchronous web-based sessions this can be done on a whiteboard, in a chat field, independently at one's desk, or via email to the facilitator, and so on.)
- **Ask:** "What will create a positive return on your investment of time in this session?"
- **Ask:** "What do you need to leave here with? Take a moment and write your answer to that on the inside cover of your workbook."
- **Say:** "Before we go further, I'd like you to determine what you are looking to take away from our time together. Please identify your WIIFM—What's In It For Me."
- **Say:** "We will be working with conflict management strategies today, so please write down two examples of conflict you are currently dealing with professionally and personally so that you can focus on how you will use the course content in your current situations."

Application

Entire books are dedicated to this component. We know learners need to put content into practice in learning events—I won't even attempt to provide an exhaustive defense for it here. Instead I will share examples of how to take content you feel compelled to insert as lecture and effectively convert it to interactive application exercises in which the content and the activity happen together. Keep in mind that the more senses learners involve in developing a new skill or acquiring new knowledge, the greater their ability will be to perform the skill or recall and apply the knowledge at a later time.

> **Insider Tip**
>
> In e-learning, lecture looks like screens full of paragraphs to read. A trainer telling learners information is replaced with slides of content "telling" learners information. Neither is good. Both are avoidable.

- **Instead of:** Building slides showing a process and scripting an explanation of the process . . .
  - **Try this:** Provide small groups with slips of paper listing steps of the process. Direct groups to arrange them in what they believe to be chronological order. Observe groups' progress and share feedback, tips, and direction as they work. Reveal the process and have them compare their work to it. Facilitate a discussion around their questions on steps they misplaced. (In e-learning this can be a drag-and-drop exercise.) Then provide a case study or scenario in which learners apply the process.
  - **Or this:** Identify a starting point and the desired end point of a process. Using butcher block paper, a whiteboard, or large sticky notes and a wall, learners identify, record, and place in chronological order the steps they take between the two points. Debrief the exercise by comparing group's output to one another and then to the actual or recommended process. (In virtual instructor-led training, or VILT, this can be done on whiteboards in breakout rooms.) Have learners create job aids of the complete process based on all of the information and then use the job aids to role play the process in prepared scenarios.

  - **Or this:** Direct participants to draw a picture of the process they follow to complete a task (for example, design a course, develop a lead, get a product to market, implement a change, write a report, give a peer feedback) and share their drawings in trios. Then introduce the recommended process and discuss discrepancies and variances. (In VILT this can be done on whiteboards in breakout rooms and the main room for the final step.)
- **Instead of:** Listing examples and non-examples in a workbook . . .
  - **Try this:** Create an out-of-seat, manipulative-based activity in which teams receive the same examples and non-examples on sticky notes and are directed to display them in two categories on a wall or flip chart. Teams then rotate to the stations looking for commonalities and differences, followed by a group discussion. (In VILT this can be done by displaying an item on screen and directing learners to use response buttons to indicate their categorizations.) Referring to the examples, learners then create project-specific examples of their own.

> **Insider Tip**
> For content-heavy subjects or existing courses, shift from pushing to pulling and from pushing to playing.

  - **Or this:** Invite learner groups to write sample examples and non-examples and present them to the large group to categorize. (In e-learning this can be achieved using a discussion board for participants.)
- **Instead of:** Lecturing on a topic . . .
  - **Try this:** Conduct multiple, simultaneous standing meetings at stations in the training room where learners interact with a chunk of the content and complete an application exercise or answer a series of questions before moving to the next station.
  - **Or this:** Move small groups into breakout rooms in a VILT session to interact with and apply a block of material (similar

to the bulleted item above) with reports from each team in the main room.

— **Or this:** Direct learners to complete the statement: "*X* [topic, skill, or action] is like __________ because __________" and connect key points of instruction to their answers.

— **Or this:** Build in moments of productive struggle. Challenge learners to figure things out on their own at first. Supplement their exploration with clues, hints, and guidance. Follow the moments of productive struggle with a rich debrief. Here are a few examples:
  - Create flash cards with a content question on one side and the answer(s) on the other side. Working in pairs, learners quiz each other by holding a card between them and alternating between asking and answering the questions.
  - Send learners on a scavenger hunt to find software features, elements of a new policy or regulation, resources available on a collaboration platform such as SharePoint, or other "treasures."

— **Or this:** Read aloud statements based on or related to the instruction (some are accurate and some are not) and direct learners to position themselves at stations in the room labelled to align with their perceptions. Then have them apply the accurate information in job-based situations. Signage ideas include:
  - Agree—Unsure—Disagree
  - True—Undecided—False
  - Current Practice/Regulation—You Made That Up!—Former Practice/Regulation

Self-Reflection

Each time I lead a learning event for instructional designers or trainers to hone their craft, when we pause the instruction to allow time for self-reflection, I consistently ask the learners if those 5 to 7 minutes were useful to them. Did taking that time increase their likelihood of using the content covered so far in the practice of their work? Universally, the answer is "yes."

Next, I point out that I asked these questions to help them see how critical it is to provide learners with this time—even when, as designers or trainers, we are feeling the pressure of squeezing in one more content piece. Resist cutting training time that is dedicated to reflection.

While it can be sufficient to simply pause and allow unstructured time for the learners to reflect, here are five structured ways as well:

- Ask learners to reconsider a challenge question posed at the opening of the program. How has their reaction to it changed—or not—based on course content?
- Allow 5 minutes for learners to review the course material covered in the previous hour, identify three actions they will take as a result, and then schedule those three things in their planners.
- Invite learners to draw an image, infographic, mindmap, or graphic organizer that summarizes their takeaways from the learning event.
- Have individuals, partners, or small teams create a Top Ten List of the most critical course content.
- In e-learning programs, insert screens asking learners to pause and consider how they will apply what has been introduced, schedule an action into their planners, and so on.

At the end of each chapter in this book, there is a section called Put It Into Practice. Look back at these activities for examples of how simple building in reflection can be.

Call to Action

A call to action is what providing training is all about—learners doing something differently after training, better than they did it before, or that they weren't doing at all. To make a change, something needs to change—by definition!

You can build a call to action into the course time, as in the following examples:

- For a time management course, have people bring their digital devices (planners, smartphones, laptops) to implement strategies introduced in class, such as adjusting auto-reminder settings, disabling notifications, setting up folders, creating rules for email, scheduling "think time," and so on).

- For a skills-based class, such as budgeting, project management, or designing learning, have participants bring a current or past project to training to work on, review, or revise.
- In a module on business writing for managers that was added to a management skills series I led, to leverage the concepts introduced in the course and align them with the add-on module, I brought boxes of thank you cards to training for them to write notes to their employees—during training time.

You can also build in calls to action as activities that take place outside of the learning event but are part of the course completion requirements. It is a mistake to assume that given effective tools and strategies, shown how to use them, and provided an opportunity to practice them that learners will make the leap to performing differently on the job. The call to action component raises the bar. It sets an expectation or asks the learner to set one. It requires on-the-job application and supports the learners in setting their own plans for it. Certainly it rises above ending learning events with "that's all folks—go be great."

The best-case scenario for a call to action is to build practical application into the course requirements. Create application assignments that require learners to return to work and use the skills as part of a structured on-the-job activity. This is not homework or self-study or reviewing case studies inspired by real work events after the training ends. This is *using* the skills practiced in the session back in reality.

Unfortunately, building this in as a course requirement is not always a decision that falls within the control of the L&D function. When you are not allowed to build in best-case-scenario calls to action or there are not enough resources available to review assignments and give feedback to learners, consider these ideas:

- Direct learners to locate an accountability accomplice. Ask them each to share with their partner one action they will take within one hour, two actions they will take within two days, and three actions they will take within three weeks. Six actions in total. Have them exchange contact information and agree to alert one another when they have taken each action.

- Structure a Continue, Stop, Start activity (similar to the one presented at the close of Chapter 1). Under Continue, learners define their current actions that the program validated are serving them. Under Stop, they identify actions that they now realize are working against them. And, under Start, they record new behaviors they are taking from the course.
- Ask individuals, partners, or small teams create a Top Ten List of ideas to implement after the course.

The six components of context, introductions with intent, goal setting, application, self-reflection, and a call to action are the bottom-line, essential elements of a time-constrained course. Be vigilant in ensuring their placement in the design. If you are wondering "Where does the content go?" it is goes into these six buckets. It will begin to surface when the context is created and introductions are facilitated. During goal setting, learners will heighten their awareness of what they need and will therefore recognize it when presented. The content will be inherent in the application exercises. Learners will lock in on the content that is most relevant and meaningful to them while reflecting, and in a call to action they will transfer the content to the job through changes in behavior. Focus on building in the six components, and the content will fall into place.

Leverage the Trainer's Function

In Chapter 5, I shared the three most influential factors in employees' success in transferring new skills to their jobs:

1. What the employees' *managers* do before the training
2. What the *trainer* does during the training
3. What the employees' *managers* do after the training

So, if the manager's role is the bread of our training sandwich, the trainer is the filling, which as everyone knows is pretty important to the sandwich experience. Here are a few ways trainers can influence the success of training (see additional trainer tips in Chapter 8):

- **Establish the value—immediately.** For fun, I searched online for "how long do you have to get a person's attention." The results were broad in terms of the medium (grab a website visitor's attention, gain attention as a public speaker, duration videos are watched). The answers I found were measured in seconds. Seconds! Just 7, 15, and 8 seconds, respectively, for websites, public speakers, and videos. There were also some interesting results on strategies to get and hold attention, articles on attention spans in classrooms (pedagogy), and tests to assess your attention span—if you find yourself with a few minutes. It seems safe to infer from this that you need to establish the WIIFM for learners right away. Where the bathrooms are located and your introduction can both be addressed after learners have determined they care.

- **Create memorable moments.** Trainers' most powerful tools to achieve memorable moments are aligning new content with learners' existing context, grounding the instruction in real-world examples that relate to the learners' specific work, sharing relevant stories to illustrate learning points, developing mental postcards for learners, and providing targeted individual feedback.
- **Employ best practices for training room management.** The short-list actions are establish and adhere to social agreements (ground rules), provide frequent breaks, put learners in the spotlight, and engage all learners.
- **Be organized and prepared.** An exceptional trainer can create a successful learning experience in the absence of a well-designed program. Unfortunately, an ill-prepared trainer can make a mess of a well-designed program too. It will not matter that the instructional designer created the perfect job aid if the trainer does not distribute it, nor will it matter that the designer created engaging application-based exercises if the trainer decides to "talk through" the material because she doesn't fully understand the activity. Trainers, make the most of well-designed training by being organized and prepared.
- **Set post-training expectations.** Although it will be between the manager and the learner to establish performance expectations, the trainer should alert learners to what to expect next. Here are a few examples to get you thinking:

— "The first time you try to *X*, don't be surprised if *Y* happens. In that event, what will your next step be?"
— "Page *X* is your planning tool. Let's take a few minutes to complete it now. Don't be surprised when your manager asks to review it with you—I have asked her to!"
— "In the coming days and weeks, be on the lookout for emails from me—I won't inundate you, but I will be reaching out. If you don't receive them, please check your spam folder and contact me if you don't see them. My contact information is. . . ."
— "This course also has an extensive set of job aids, resources, and additional self-paced challenge activities. They are all available on the LMS (or Dropbox folder or other medium) I set up. . . ."

In addition to designing and developing engaging learning based on a sound analysis, here are ways instructional designers can support trainers to achieve those things:

- **Provide options.** When you build facilitative flexibility into the design, you establish boundaries for trainers to work within and bring their style to the event, while remaining true to your design. Here are a few ways to do that:
  — Mark select activities as optional, allowing trainers to tailor the delivery to accommodate learners' needs without disturbing the integrity of the design.
  — Offer sample stories trainers can use when they don't have their own.
  — Provide alternative activities to accommodate unforeseen constraints. Examples of unexpected constraints might include any of the following: the class size differs from the expectation; the training space is not conducive to a planned exercise; technology challenges prevent a VILT activity from working; or outside influences such as emergency drills, extreme weather, or daylight savings time and time zone disconnects interfere with activity flow due to learners arriving at various times, especially in VILT sessions.

- **Make it easy to be prepared.** Providing a comprehensive and easy-to-navigate facilitator guide is critical. Without one, trainers won't likely adhere to your plan. Consider these best practices:
  - — List preparation steps at the front of the guide (what to pack, pre-training emails to send, setup guidelines, and so on).
  - — Use lean text and bullet points for quick reference.
  - — Add prompts for story sharing, checking for understanding, debriefs, and such.
  - — Provide clear, concise activity instructions and embedded answer keys.
  - — Break down timing cues for blocks of time to indicate allocations for introducing the activity, learner preparation for the exercise, activity time, and debriefing.
- **Make it easy to be organized.** Trainers have a lot going on. Everything you do to make their lives easier in relation to your course will translate into increased chances of them adhering to your design. Try some of these ideas to help:
  - — Provide trainers with a kit of prepared manipulatives and resources needed to facilitate activities.
  - — Set up and follow a simple file naming convention for electronic resources trainers will use. Be sure files display sequentially by using double digits for 01, 02, 03 and so on.
  - — Double check, and then triple check, internal references in materials created for the trainer.
  - — Conduct hand-off sessions with trainers to orient them to the course design, their responsibilities that are unique to the course, and the resources you are providing to them when a formal train-the-trainer event is not planned.
- **Build trainers' tools first.** Reality check: Is a facilitator guide the last item you develop for a course—if you create one at all? Often, designers place priority on building the materials learners receive. This is all wrong. Process trumps content, and process resides in facilitator guides. Besides, you *can* give a learner a blank piece of paper (some argue you should, in fact), but you can't give a trainer a blank book and expect them to recognize, understand, or adhere to your design.

As an instructional designer, you may wonder how Broad and Newstrom's findings on the trainer's role in supporting transfer of learning apply to e-learning or other self-paced instruction in which there is no trainer (Broad & Newstrom 1992). I certainly cannot speak on their behalf, but I do like to interpret—extrapolate even—their work this way: In self-paced learning, the design of the module stands in place of the trainer. It takes on the role and responsibility of providing the learner with an engaging, meaningful, thought-provoking, and action-inducing learning event. And that means it is your responsibility, as the instructional designer, to build these features into your course designs.

Final Thoughts

Listening isn't learning. (Let that be your mantra as an instructional designer or trainer!)

Put It Into Practice

Considering the examples and ideas presented in this chapter, how will you shift to being an information miner? What content do your course designs currently provide that could be mined instead?

Get specific. Choose a course and record the content pieces it is pushing out (providing) to learners in the left column of the chart on the next page. For each, identify and record in the right column an approach you can use to pull (mine) it from learners instead.

Pushing:	Pull by:

Chapter Actions

- ❑ Self-assess how well you are maximizing limited training time using the instrument in Chapter 10.
- ❑ Implement the "pull" strategies you identified in the Put It Into Practice activity.
- ❑ For each learning activity you plan, ask yourself: "Does this activity push or pull?"
- ❑ Shift from cataloguing information for learners to developing learning experiences that engage and require learner participation—not as optional but as fundamental to the course design.
- ❑ Build practical strategies into your courses instead of theoretical content.
- ❑ Cross-check your designs to confirm that you have integrated the six essential components: context, introductions with intent, goal setting, application, self-reflection, and a call to action.
- ❑ Build your trainer tools first, not last.
- ❑ Revisit your chapter-by-chapter action plan in Chapter 10 and update it with actions related to the content of this chapter.

7

How Do I Take Training Beyond the Training Room?

Five Touchpoints to Cut Training Time, Not Contact Time

Why don't employees use what they learn? It is true that fundamental errors in the design and delivery of training can prevent transfer of learning, including errors such as: the instructional designer's upfront analysis was inaccurate or not conducted; the course presented theory instead of providing practical techniques; the design employed more "push" (via lecture, data dumps, and extensive manuals) than "pull" (via exploration, collaboration, practice, feedback, and activity workbooks); or any number of other issues. These mistakes hinder even the motivated participant's ability to learn and ultimately apply learning.

But let's look past these errors and think of your own training experiences. What has prevented you from making changes you were inspired to make, wanted to make, and planned to make? Consider, and add to, this list:

- ❑ Changing was harder than anticipated, and your initial attempts were unsuccessful.
- ❑ There was no time in the day with the volume of work and "catch up" awaiting you after training to try new things.

- ❑ Even though you modified your behavior, no one noticed or acknowledged it—so you reverted to old habits.
- ❑ The coaching, support, and feedback received in training were absent on the job.
- ❑ Self-doubt undermined your confidence in your ability to apply the skills.
- ❑ Unrelenting work demands and turnaround times caused too much stress to experiment with using new techniques.
- ❑ Work became a distraction causing you to lose sight of your implementation plans.
- ❑ Transitioning from the training room's "safe space" for applying the new skills to the "hostile" reality of the workplace was too great to surmount.
- ❑ ______________________________
- ❑ ______________________________
- ❑ ______________________________

Looking at the list, it is easy to see that learners are up against a lot when they leave training. There are so many potential and logical reasons for them to relapse into existing, long-standing habits. Chapters 5 and 6 provided strategies to begin building a development continuum *before* the training event and *during* it. In this chapter, we extend those efforts to encompass the golden hours (and days and weeks and months) *after* the training, because during that time there is a great deal you can do to remove obstacles for learners—or at least set them at the side of the road.

Touchpoints—Your Key to Taking Training Beyond the Training Room

Creating the learning event isn't the end of the design role. Without reinforcement, application, measurement, recognition, support, coaching, and so on, the well-designed learning event will be hard-pressed to change employees' behavior on its own. Building a successful learning event is critical, of course, but the development continuum concept we have been discussing requires you to build additional elements too. Ideally, you will create a series of varied touchpoints that participants will receive from multiple contacts, at multiple times, through multiple channels. Touchpoints unlock the door that constricts learning to "an event that happens in the training room" and elevate learning to become part of the organizational culture. We will look at 40 ideas in five categories of touchpoints:

- ✓ After-training communication campaign elements
- ✓ Job-embedded application activities
- ✓ Learning boosters
- ✓ Manager support strategies and tools
- ✓ Evaluation strategies

(Note: To rate yourself on how well you are reclaiming post-training time, check out the assessment in Chapter 10.)

Leverage After-Training Communication Campaign Elements

The communication campaign was introduced in Chapter 5. If you did not skip ahead to this section when you created yours, you will want to revisit your draft plan now and add critical post-training elements to it. Here is a list to inspire your thoughts for post-training communication:

- **Ghost-write emails for trainers to send to participants after training.** Just as the pre-training emails you drafted for trainers set a tone for the event, the follow-up emails you write should support a positive post-training mindset. Here are a few ideas for you to choose from based on factors such as organizational culture, learner profile, rigor of course content, and so on:
  - **Motivational messages:** Provide an encouraging word, a success story, or the benefits to the learner (that you included in the pre-training emails).
  - **Reminder messages:** Reinforce a critical takeaway, highlight key points of the curriculum, recap essential content, or provide job aids or a course-summary infographic. (You can create infographics with tools such as piktochart.com and canva.com.)

- **Master-practitioner messages:** Provide a succinct set of best practice tips for implementation from one who has walked in the learners' shoes.
- **Would-you-look-at-that messages:** Share timely content that is connected to the course, such as trending videos, articles from trade publications, research findings that validate course content, or even a national news story that highlights the WIIFM (such as "let's not be the next one in the news for this"), and so on.
- **Next-step messages:** Prepare participants for what to expect or direct them on actions to take.

Be prepared for potential resistance when you ask trainers to add communicating with learners post-training to their job function. Overcome that resistance by making it easy for them—provide e-copies of the messages, highlight content they will need to tailor (greeting, signature line, course cohort) and other sections they may want to edit, and encourage them to set calendar reminders for sending the emails. You may even leverage a social media platform for trainers to distribute the messages through, letting them take advantage of features that allow for scheduling communications to be sent at designated times.

- **Ghost-write emails for managers to send to participants after training.** The focus of these messages will be on structuring a post-training framework for success and implementing the newly acquired skills and knowledge. The timing of these messages will be critical:
  - **Upon return from training—to establish a framework:** Keep this email short. Include a welcome back component, an invitation to meet within 48 hours, and an acknowledgement that the employees' schedules will need space to apply the learning. The emphasis of this email should be on the learning and providing support for employees to bring the new skills into their work routine instead of focusing on how much they were missed and all the work that awaits them now that they are back.

  - **Within two weeks of training—to keep the employee encouraged:** This email is intended to acknowledge the learners' efforts in implementing the learning. It should include praise, specifics on the behaviors or actions observed, the manager's encouragement to continue, and an offer of support to enhance their progress. Your draft of this message will need to include multiple fill-in-the-blank components for the manager to customize. And, it may be accompanied by a manager's job aid that includes "look fors"—as in "what to look for" in employees' actions after training—to guide the manager in tailoring the message.
- **Prime learner-led social media discussions with discussion board posts.** Chapter 5's section on enticing and exciting learners prior to training included creating learner-driven discussion areas using social media or your LMS. This tool, if developed, can be leveraged as a post-training communication element too. Craft questions the learners can reply to, ask how they are using the skills on the job, post content that can spark debate, set up a discussion chain for sharing their successes and stumbles with one another, request feedback, and so on.

Create Job-Embedded Application Activities

Technically, this strategy will be a part of your program design when you create multi-session courses; therefore, it is referenced in Chapter 6's Call to Action section, but it is also listed here for two reasons: first, job-embedded application activities reclaim after-session time for continued development; and second, they take learning into the workplace, which is a key step in changing behavior and establishing new habits.

The cynics refer to job-embedded application as "homework," but it isn't. Homework is about drills, fictitious situations, and "what would you do if *X*" scenarios. By requiring participants to use a skill introduced in training at work, record the outcomes of their efforts, and receive feedback when they return to the next training session, job-embedded application assignments narrow the gap between a supportive, feedback-rich learning environment and independent application in their work environment. Here are some examples:

- Learners in an effective selling skills course use a technique introduced for matching customer needs with products to develop solutions for prospective clients. They bring their analysis, proposed solutions, and results of their efforts to the next session to share and receive feedback on.
- In a behavioral interviewing program, participants choose an open position, identify job competencies, and write behavioral-based questions that align with them. If there are no current job openings, they base the assignment on their own position or a frequently-hired-for position. In the second session, participants role-play interviews using their drafted questions and revise them as needed based on feedback.
- In a course on safety awareness, participants assess their work environment for potential hazards identified in the training, rectify them, and document the actions taken.
- Participants attending a process improvement course can be asked to choose a process they own, assess its effectiveness, modify or redesign it based on course principles, and present their process improvement to the large group in a subsequent session for input and critique.

In a nutshell, job-embedded assignments provide a reason for learners to demonstrate new skills while performing their jobs.

Trigger Action With Learning Boosters

Just as vaccination booster shots periodically boost an immune system, learning boosters infuse participants' post-training day-to-day with a renewed focus on their learning. Learning boosters can be easy and relatively quick to implement. Or, they can be easy and a bit more orchestrated to implement. Either way, they should always be easy. If they aren't—they won't happen.

You can embed select learning boosters into post-training email communications (discussed above) and have others as standalone components of the overall development continuum. When they are embedded, the existing distribution channel will simplify things. When they stand independently, they create another opportunity to bring development out of the training room and into the workplace. In both instances, they renew participants' focus on the skill sets and desired behaviors introduced in the learning event.

Although any training reminder, including emails, can serve as a trigger to reignite learners' commitment to taking action, you are encouraged to develop learning boosters with greater engagement in mind. Here are some ideas of what that might look like: The learner can engage with the material through an independent activity, with other learners, with members of the training team, or with their manager. Let this list inspire your thinking on the booster tools and processes you will build and distribute to learners:

Trigger Action With Learning Boosters

Have you ever committed to do something only to have it slip your mind? Then, days or weeks later, a passing comment, commercial, or other trigger reminds you of it? And, even though you had every intention of following through, without the trigger it wouldn't have happened?

Learners experience the same phenomenon—even in the best-case scenario, in which they appreciate the learning opportunity, arrive motivated, value the material, and intend to use it. When they return to work, they get hit by all that transpired while they were in training and often lose sight of their implementation plans. Learning boosters can refocus them on their action plans and implementation strategies.

- **In the days following training.** Aim to create low-threshold touchpoints that keep the training experience at the forefront of the learners' minds without a significant demand on their time. Ideally, the invitation to access these boosters or the encouragement to complete them will occur two to three days after attending training. (Note: The day after training is commonly a catchup day, and by four days out, learners may have moved on mentally. That is why the two to three days is optimal timing.) Consider these examples of low-threshold touchpoints:

— Using a provided instrument, learners compare their own work process to the model introduced in learning. (Distribute the instrument after training instead of at the end of the event to derive the "booster" benefit.)
— Learners schedule an initial post-training checkpoint with their managers to share their learning experience, intended implementation plans, and requested manager support. This discussion can be guided by tools you create and distribute to both parties (see sample instruments for both the manager and the employee in Chapter 10). The tools can include recommended outcomes for the conversation, planning worksheets for the learner, and guiding questions for the manager.
— Learners reassess their knowledge retention by completing an online quiz of application-based test questions, playing a game-show-format exercise in which their scores are compared with other players, or another knowledge check.
— Using a provided instrument, learners create a job-based action plan. In-class action planning may have occurred, but after returning to their workspace and completing an environmental scan or an inventory of their strengths and deficits, participants' action planning will be informed by both the course content and their work reality.

- **In the weeks following training.** Since some time has passed, the learning boosters scheduled for a few weeks after training should dive deeper—reconnect the learner to the strategies, support their implementation efforts, allow them to assess their proficiency in applying them, or even provide a reality check on their implementation progress. Here are some ideas:
— Learners assess their skills application proficiency in a work situation. This can be done by responding to a bank of reflective questions distributed via e-survey, completing an after-action assessment tool, or comparing their performance against a checklist, to name a few approaches.
— Following a guided process, learners engage in peer-to-peer exchanges. This booster can actually be initiated during the learning event by asking learners to choose an accountability

accomplice or training buddy; they exchange contact information and commit to complete self-determined actions by a specified date. Knowing their partners will be expecting an update can increase implementation rates.

- — Learners schedule a second post-training check-in with their managers to share an update on implementation results, any roadblocks encountered, additional or different support requests, as well as any new insights they have developed in the past weeks while implementing their plans.
- — Also think about how to leverage the tiny training components (discussed in Chapter 5) that you created or can create to extend the learning. Gamified activities can go a long way to reengage learners with the content and increase their day-to-day awareness of their related behaviors. You can even reward learners who complete learning booster activities with a transfer of learning tool—a gadget or useful workplace item imprinted with a key course reminder—that, when they see it regularly, will remind them to apply the content.

- **In the months following training.** If your course evaluation plan includes measuring behavior change (Level 3 evaluation in Kirkpatrick's model, which we will touch on later in this chapter), you would typically conduct this measure about 8 to 12 weeks after training, right about when you'd introduce your final learning booster (Kirkpatrick & Kirkpatrick 2006). Even if your organization does not have the resources to conduct a formal Level 3 assessment, you may be able to gather informal data on behavior change and anecdotal examples with some of these learning booster ideas:
  - — Create opportunities for learners to come together with other interested learners to practice skills, share best practices, clarify processes or models after attempting to follow them, receive feedback on performance, collaborate to resolve challenges faced, and so on. These can be trainer-led, department leader-led, or learner-led by volunteers. To also capture self-reported Level 3 indicators in these events, provide tools for recording application examples. A graffiti station when they

arrive, for example, posing the question "What have you done with *X* lately?" invites informal data collection.

— Learners use a provided tool to reflect on and record their training implementation accomplishments in the months since participating in the course. The instrument you provide can include prompts of the topics, strategies, tools, and processes introduced in the course to guide the learner. The data recorded here could be shared with the manager, inform the employee's performance review, or even be shared with L&D as anecdotal, self-reported Level 3 indicators.

— Create packages to enable managers and department leads to integrate a "spotlight on training" segment in their existing staff meetings. These can range from learner-led teach backs, success story highlights, or fun activities and challenges that are manipulative-based, to discussion questions for meeting leaders or scavenger hunts for meeting members directing them to recall and share recent workplace situations in which the course skills were used.

Deploy Manager Support Strategies and Tools

Chapter 5 introduced the idea that successful training requires a manager sandwich. What managers do after employees attend training creates the trifecta. You will recall the three most influential factors in employees successfully transferring new skills to the job:

1. What the employees' *managers* do before the training (addressed in Chapter 5)
2. What the *trainer* does during the training (addressed in Chapter 6)
3. What the employees' *managers* do after the training

So, what sorts of things can a manager do post-learning? Here are some ideas to consider:

- Inquire about the learning event and employees' takeaways from it.
- Provide support for employees post-training.

- Watch for behaviors after training that were established as expectations before training.
- Continue to manage employees' workloads and assignments so they have the necessary time to implement new behaviors—which can take additional time initially.

The following are actions you can take, as an instructional designer, that will enhance a manager's post-training effectiveness as a partner to the learning process:

- **Clue managers in on the learning continuum.** Share reminders with managers that true development requires a before-, during-, and after-the-learning-event continuum. Their functions post-training will include helping employees reenter their roles, allowing them to stumble without harsh consequences as they apply new behaviors, encouraging them to share learning with other employees, and so on.
- **Ask managers to create space for employees to apply new learning.** Protect post-training application time by specifically asking managers to create space for employees to implement their action plans. This may include continuing to reassign certain responsibilities temporarily after the learning event.
- **Provide managers with "look for" checklists.** These can be both desired behaviors (to acknowledge, encourage, and reinforce) as well as common missteps (to redirect and coach employees through).
- **Keep managers in the loop.** Copy managers on post-training emails to participants from the trainer, communications that introduce learning boosters, and so on.
- **Encourage carrots.** Encourage managers to offer rewards, special acknowledgments, and preferred assignments to employees who demonstrate new, desired behaviors after training.
- **Go digital.** Create an online platform specifically for managers to support one another and share successes. This could be on your LMS or on a site such as Yammer, Socialcast, or another platform your organization uses.

- **Educate managers on the key role they play in successful transfer of learning.** Help them discover the behaviors they can demonstrate that will enhance employees' successes with their new skills. These behaviors include:
  - **Be patient.** Learners will require time and a safe environment to develop their proficiency with new skills. How initial failures are managed will heavily affect the employees' next steps.
  - **Acknowledge how difficult change can be.** When employees hear their manager say that new behaviors will feel different—even uncomfortable—after training, their resilience is strengthened. They may also feel more comfortable coming to their manager for coaching and feedback as they work to develop new habits.
  - **Revisit goals set with employees before training.** Prior to training, clear expectations of increased performance were established. Now, those expectations can be reviewed, clarified, and have specificity added to them as necessary.
  - **Be more flexible about turnaround times for tasks.** Performing job functions in a new way will likely require additional time at first. When managers ask employees to adhere to pre-training turnaround times, employees may actually hear: "Revert back to old processes and pre-training behaviors so we don't interrupt operations."
  - **Plan for relapses.** By anticipating relapses in behavior and proactively setting a strategy for managing them, it will be easier for employees to renew their commitment to behavior change.
  - **Create application opportunities.** Find and create job-relevant opportunities for employees to practice the new skills. By immediately assigning such projects, the gap between learning and applying will be reduced. Managers will also want to ensure employees have the technology and resources required to implement new approaches.
  - **Provide feedback and praise.** To sustain employees' efforts to use new skills on the job, managers will want to give

immediate positive reinforcement. They will also want to watch for acknowledging and course-correcting opportunities in employees' actions.

— **Be a role model.** Demonstrating the skills sends a strong message and creates an example to emulate. This strategy can extend to partnering employees with other role models as well by connecting them with mentors or encouraging networking with other program participants.

Build Evaluation Into Your Project Plans

Employees do what gets measured. Although there are all sorts of benefits to evaluating learning—showing achievement of organizational goals and effectiveness of the learning solution, demonstrating your value to the organization, and marketing courses to future participants using data gathered, among others—here, we will look at how measuring learning can help transfer the learning. And that is your ultimate goal when you design a course—improving human performance.

As background to the information that follows, here is a brief overview of Kirkpatrick's Four Levels of Evaluation (Kirkpatrick & Kirkpatrick 2006):

Level 1—Reaction	What do participants think of the event and what are their intentions to use the course materials and strategies?
Level 2—Knowledge	What have participants learned in this event? (Be mindful that *pre-* and post-measures will help validate that the learning can be attributed to the event, and valid instruments are required too.)
Level 3—Behavior	What are participants doing differently on the job as a result of what they learned in the training?
Level 4—Results	What has the organization realized as a result of the behavior changes participants have made in their on-the-job performance?

With this understanding of Kirkpatrick's model, let's now see how measuring learning can help transfer the learning. Evaluation will help you:

- **Send a signal that "this" matters.** When participants realize that no one of authority cares enough to be concerned with assessing the impact of training, it is reasonable for them to question why they should. Evaluation is L&D's secret weapon. Given the demands on employees' limited time, it is understandable that many will prioritize the actions and outcomes they will be measured against—during performance reviews, salary negotiations, interviews for promotional opportunities, and so on. When training gets measured, it also gets more attention from participants.

  Worth mentioning here is the Hawthorne Effect. Admittedly, it is based on research participation versus learning measurement, but the parallel of assessing adult's work performance creates a compelling case for evaluating learning. Employees at the Western Electric telephone manufacturing factory in Hawthorne, Illinois, were studied to determine if changes to their work environment, such as lighting levels, would affect their productivity. And, they did. But employees' productivity increased *both* when lighting was enhanced and when it was diminished, as well as when other changes were made, leading to the conclusion that the influential factor was the observation, not the environmental changes. This effect was documented in the 1920s and 1930s and has been the subject of further analysis ever since (McCambridge, Wilton, & Elbourne 2013).
- **Support learners in building self-confidence.** If employees lack confidence in a new skill, it is more likely they will be timid about using the skill at work. There is a sign on the wall in my gym that reads: "The body can only achieve what the mind believes," and it seems applicable here too. A well-crafted Level 2 instrument, deployed during the learning event, can address insecurity head on. By showing learners where their strengths and gaps may be, Level 2 instruments position learners to close

their gaps during the learning event through a heightened awareness of the gaps, asking questions, taking risks in practice activities, requesting feedback, and so on.

- **Encourage on-the-job performance.** The job-embedded activities, discussed previously in this chapter, raise the bar on expectations for employees "doing something" with new skills. You can go further to motivate on-the-job performance through formal evaluation initiatives that track and gather data on how much training employees are applying at key intervals after participating (typically 8 to 12 weeks). When there are limits on your evaluation abilities, consider surveying participants 60 or 90 days after training to assess perceptions of how the course is influencing their workplace effectiveness. Although this is not a classic Level 3 evaluation, which can be challenging to implement, it will give an indication of employees' opinions of how the skills are being used. This data can inform what support tools or job aids may be appreciated and used if provided, and it can also identify opportunities to offer supplemental learning or refresher sessions.

Final Thoughts

Employees need a post-training environment that supports transfer of learning. The learners' managers, the trainer, and the learners themselves will have the greatest responsibility in achieving the transfer, but your support actions can play a critical role as well. Begin with envisioning a development continuum and then build the tools it requires. Be sure to educate all the parties—managers, trainers, learners—on their responsibilities associated with transfer of learning and on the tools and processes you have created to facilitate the development continuum.

Put It Into Practice

There are 40 some touchpoint strategies in this chapter. If you apply the Pareto Principle to them (the 80/20 Rule), about 8 of the 40, when implemented, will have the greatest impact on your learners and organization. So, find and list here your Crazy Eight—those that will derive the most significant benefit for you:

My Crazy Eight

1.	5.
2.	6.
3.	7.
4.	8.

As powerful as the actions you just listed may be, some may be challenging. So, supplement that list with the low-hanging fruit—the items you have the authority and means to develop and implement. Let's call it your "Why Aren't I Already Doing These Things?" list:

Why Aren't I Already Doing These Things?

1.
2.
3.
4.
5.

Chapter Actions

- ❑ Self-assess how well you are reclaiming post-training time using the instrument in Chapter 10.
- ❑ Build a complete communication campaign, or revise the one you started after Chapter 5 to include post-training elements.
- ❑ Revisit your course design to determine where job-embedded application activities can be introduced.
- ❑ Create at least one—preferably three—learning boosters for your course. It is okay to reach for low-hanging fruit at this time if learning boosters are new to you and your organization. It is more about creating the culture of post-training boosters than it is about dazzling with them—at first anyway!
- ❑ Determine your best options for informing managers of and educating them on their post-training support roles.
- ❑ Assess how you are currently using evaluation to strategically encourage on-the-job application and make revisions or enhancements as your authority and influence allow.
- ❑ Revisit your chapter-by-chapter action plan in Chapter 10 and update it with actions related to the content of this chapter.

8

What Makes Training Great?

Part One: Demystifying What Causes It

Part Two: Influencing It From Your Non-Designer Role

It isn't easy to create effective learning events. If it were easy, there would be little need for instructional designers—everyone would build their own learning events. If it were easy, there would be no water-cooler talk about training experiences with witticisms such as "Death by PowerPoint," "How to Get the Most From a Lecture—Nap," and "You Are Scheduled for Training—and Other Scary Workplace Phrases." You get the idea.

It is not that creating effective learning events is so difficult either—but you do need to have the right tools. Here is a quick story to illustrate my point. I was considering buying a boat. Having found one that fit my needs, I made an offer, scheduled a survey, and showed up for the survey full of excitement. As the engine surveyor and I poked around in the engine compartment, the hull surveyor arrived with his moisture meter in hand. Although I had been on the boat multiple times with a knowledgeable friend who has decades of boating industry experience, neither of us owns a moisture meter. Gary, with his meter, knew in minutes what we weren't able to figure out after days on the boat—the hull was full of water. When you have the right tool and the knowledge of how to use it, determining if a boat is water logged is easy—yet a complete mystery to the rest of us. And that is what Part One of this chapter is about—providing you with a starter tool kit needed to demystify what causes training to be great.

Part Two will shift into practical, actionable strategies for you to make a positive impact on a learning event's effectiveness and participants' perceptions of it—regardless of your role in the process.

Part One: Welcome to the Beginning!

If you jumped ahead to this chapter, good choice! There is a body of knowledge and a model for building effective training that anyone who designs or leads training sessions should be aware of and allow to guide their actions. Entire books are dedicated to them. And for good reason—they are that foundational to the goal of effective workplace training. Here, we are going to provide an essentials overview to two of them:

- ✓ Adult learner characteristics
- ✓ The classic instructional systems design model, ADDIE

If you have been exposed to this content before, let Part One of this chapter serve as a touchstone for you. It is common, once we become proficient at performing a task, to lose sight of the basics. Revisiting the fundamentals periodically can help ensure you don't stray too far from the foundational principles that make training great.

If these are new to you, the following pages will help inform your reading of the rest of the book. They may even increase your confidence as a learning professional or partner. In the Introduction of the book, I acknowledged that there is a reason you are in the role you are in. Your credentials, experience, natural inclination—or all three—contributed to where you are in relation to building training. The following concepts can validate your instincts and minimize the self-doubt and indecision that often accompany making design choices. And that will save you design and development time—you will know what works and why. No more guess work.

What Adults Need From and Bring to Learning Events—Adult Learner Characteristics

Your Word of the Day is *andragogy,* which was popularized by Malcolm Knowles in *The Adult Learner: A Neglected Species* (Knowles 1984). What do you already know of andragogy? The term refers to the art and science of teaching adults, whose needs differ in many (but not all) ways from children's. Pedagogy, by distinction, relates to instructing children. Here are six characteristics of adult learners that Knowles noted in his work:

- Adults need to know why learning something is important before they learn it.
- Adults have a concept of self and do not like others imposing their wills on them.
- Adults have a wealth of knowledge and experience and want that knowledge to be recognized.
- Adults open up to learning when they think that the learning will help them with real problems.
- Adults want to know how the learning will help them immediately.
- Adults learn in response to internal (versus external) motivations.

Please read that list again. You want to be able to recite these characteristics. You also want to ensure your designs—or deliveries—honor them.

It is not enough to know the characteristics; you need to act on them as well. So, what will your awareness of these six points cause you to do differently going forward? If you have just begun reading and are not sure how to answer that question right now, answer it anyway. And take solace in knowing that Chapters 5, 6, and, 7 provide specific strategies to enhance your list. If you have already read those chapters, take a moment and reflect on how the strategies that you resonated with, that you highlighted, or that you put into your action plan align with the six characteristics.

Now, compare your list to these design and delivery actions:

- ❑ Provide learners with practical instruction instead of theoretical concepts.
- ❑ Center instruction on tools that minimize participants' pain points.
- ❑ Ensure course content is immediately applicable.
- ❑ Build processes that draw out learners' existing knowledge base.

- ❑ Integrate multiple interactive methods, including group learning, video, case studies, brainstorming, simulations, quizzes, independent reflection, role plays, and so on.
- ❑ Choose activity over lecture.
- ❑ Choose self-directed activity over highly prescribed, "follow me" type activity.
- ❑ Create opportunities for learners to experiment.
- ❑ Provide opportunities for learners to succeed.
- ❑ Allow sufficient time to debrief activities.
- ❑ Provide specific feedback to learners.

And, in your delivery, be sure to:

- ❑ Engage learners immediately.
- ❑ Promote interpersonal connections among participants.
- ❑ Support participants in identifying their unique *internal* motivators to learn (external motivators include earn credit, complete a mandatory requirement, meet an individual development plan goal, obtain a certificate, and so on.) (See Chapter 6 for ideas on creating context and individual goal setting during learning events.)
- ❑ Relate new material to learners' existing knowledge.
- ❑ Protect learners from becoming overwhelmed.
- ❑ Prioritize participants' ownership of the learning over your potential desire to be perceived as an expert (a funny thing happens when you do—their perception of you is elevated!)
- ❑ Create mental images for learners using stories, metaphors, analogies, and even your best stick figure drawings—you don't need to be an artist to leave learners with memorable visualizations.
- ❑ Intersperse dedicated time for self-reflection and implementation planning.
- ❑ Provide frequent breaks and out-of-seat learning moments.

A Framework to Organize Your Efforts–ADDIE

ADDIE is an instructional systems design (ISD) model with five phases: analysis, design, development, implementation, and evaluation. It is not the only ISD model, but its phases are represented in the elements of every model I have worked with on various projects.

Because the first three ADDIE elements—analysis, design, and development—are commonly misunderstood, I use an analogy of building a home when explaining them in classes for instructional designers. It goes like this: If you were having a custom home built, analysis would involve the designer finding out how you like to live and what you need from a home. Do you enjoy entertaining? Are you a media buff wanting an in-home theatre? Are you looking to grow your family? How important is outdoor space? In instructional design, this phase is identifying the desired business outcome—what will success look like? What does your project sponsor want to see employees doing differently on the job after successfully participating in your training? Answers to these questions will describe what your course design must achieve—and by extension, what will create a happy customer. ADDIE's analysis phase is often overlooked—mostly because new designers don't know it exists. An incomplete or nonexistent analysis phase is a grave mistake.

> **Insider Tip**
> Most frst-time instructional designers skip the beginning–mostly because they don't know it is there.

The distinction between ADDIE's design and development phases gets murky for many instructional designers. In our home building analogy, the outputs of the design phase are the architect's renderings of the home—the elevation and floorplan. These show what the finished product will look like, what rooms will be included, where they will be positioned relative to one another, how many square feet will be allocated to each, and so on. Development, however, is when tradesmen arrive onsite, pour foundations, lay pipe, hammer nails into boards, and so on—they build the home.

Back to you now, as an instructional designer, your design is the blueprint of the class. What active elements will be in it, how are they organized, what time will be allocated to each, and so on. Like the architect's drawings—which have enough detail to allow others to build the house conceived in the plan—your course design should be defined well enough that a peer could build—develop—the course from it. While the house is the output of development in the analogy, your development deliverables include participant materials, facilitator materials, visual aids, assessments, job aids, manager support tools, activity manipulatives, wall charts, course descriptions, and so on. Just as most people would not want a carpenter to begin nailing boards together before the architect completed the design, you will be well advised to design your program before you begin developing it. Again, design is creating the plan and development is building it.

The remaining ADDIE phases are implementation and evaluation. To continue the analogy, implementation—rolling out your course for learners to participate in—roughly equates to moving into the house. In training, evaluation can take on many forms. In the analogy, they can be compared to the quality of the construction and design (formative evaluation), as well as to the homeowners' first impression of the house, how well they know what is required to maintain it, how they end up using the house, and the effect their home-based lifestyle has on their lives overall (summative evaluation).

In Figure 8-1, I share the critical instructional design actions to be performed in each phase of ADDIE.

Figure 8-1. A Quick Guide to the Actions of ADDIE

Analyze–Determine business goals, performance goals, the tasks and competencies required to achieve them, as well as unique project factors and constraints, such as learner characterisitcs, timeline, and budget.

Design–Write learning objectives, choose an instructional approach, and outline the course activities and timings.

Develop–Create the learning materials required to support the course design (participant, facilitator, and manager materials; assessment tools; in-training manipulatives; job aids; and so on).

Implement–Roll out the training initiative, whether delivering face-to-face or VILT or providing learners with access to self-paced or asynchronous programs.

Evaluate–Assess achievement of desired goals for the learning solution (summative evaluation) and conduct quality-assurance throughout the ADDIE process to improve the solution you create (formative evaluation).

Part Two: So, You're Not a Designer—What Does All This Mean to You?

If you are not creating the course but are collaborating with an instructional designer, there is still a lot you can do to positively influence the outcome. In this part of the chapter, you will learn about what the instructional designer needs from you, how you can make her life easier, and how you can save yourself time in the process by getting it right the first time. If you are a SME or trainer taking on instructional design responsibilities for the first time, or on the fly in a training room, there are specific strategies on the following pages to help with those situations too.

Part Two is structured around these sections:

- ✓ The HR intermediary's role.
- ✓ The manager's role.
- ✓ The SME's role.
- ✓ The trainer's role.
- ✓ Trainer hacks for condensing training on the fly.

The HR Intermediary's Role

Like a matchmaker, your role as an HR professional may be to bring people together but not accompany them on their dinner date. However, even the matchmaker sets expectations, may establish boundaries, and can serve as an objective third party to the courting couple. Here are some actions you can take to ensure a successful union:

- **Set expectations with the project requestor.** Learning and development is not the sole responsibility of the L&D team. While they are highly instrumental in the process, sustained behavior change and employees' long-term growth and development requires engagement by the business unit, before and after the training. Equally true, the business unit will have multiple roles in scoping, creating, and implementing the learning event, including setting course expectations, providing resources to the instructional designer, clarifying content, confirming content accuracy, and performing administrative functions, to name a few. Be clear with the project requestor that they will have multiple roles to fulfill.

- **Be an advocate of the process.** You have this resource in your hands—you are informed. Support the instructional designer in discussions with your internal customers when debates arise or your project sponsors look to you to confirm or deny the instructional designer's position.
- **Encourage accountability.** All parties should be held accountable for deliverables, timelines, follow through, and so on. If the instructional designer does not raise the need for establishing communication protocols, timelines, action plans with responsibilities assigned, and other critical elements, you can introduce them into the discussion.
- **Be an informed resource.** Take a big-picture approach—you may be the only one involved with the project who knows what other relevant organizational initiatives are under way, what resources are available, what other training this should align to, what the project history is, or what land mines might exist (scheduling, resources, organizational politics, or others) that will need to be avoided.
- **Track project progress.** As the matchmaker would follow up, obtain insight, and offer feedback and guidance to the couple, you can do the same with the training initiative. Performing this role can add a sense of urgency, keep the project on the front burner, prevent increased project expense, and reduce disconnects in the final design. When a project has false starts or multiple delays, it is easy for the instructional designer to lose connection with it. The loss of connection translates to additional time being required to "get back into it" and increased likelihood of errors in the final product.

The Manager's Role

So much of what you do, don't do, or refuse to do will have direct and significant impact on the effectiveness of the training created. If you'd like to develop a bit of empathy for the instructional designer (your expert in course design) with whom you will be collaborating, consider finding eight minutes to watch the short comedy sketch "The Expert" video on YouTube: https://www.youtube.com/watch?v=BKorP55Aqvg.

And then follow this guidance:

- **Care!** You are reading this book, so I assume you already do. But managers who don't care see training as a box to check, which results in lackluster, stale training solutions that are actually a colossal waste of effort, time, and money. If what you are looking for from this book is to learn how to check the box more quickly, I have a simple solution: Cancel the training initiative—everyone's time will be better spent doing other things.
- **Be realistic.** Training is critical to developing employees and enhancing behaviors—just as a coach is to a football team's success. But, alone, without a team of players, the coach won't be able to win games. To achieve all it can, a learning event needs to be a part of a development continuum, and that continuum will require a support system. Recognize that training is not a magic bullet that "fixes" employees—in a few hours.
- **Be ready to contribute more than you thought**. Bringing in an instructional designer isn't the same as delegating a task. There will be front-end analysis data she needs from you—information and answers you may not readily have, decisions to be made, expectations to be set, resources to be provided, material to be clarified, content accuracy to be confirmed, administrative functions to perform, and more. Go in "eyes open." There will also be requests made of you once the course is developed, as discussed below and in Chapters 5 and 7, and these will be critical.
- **Be prepared to be pressed more than you thought**. Telling the instructional designer "I need the employees to learn *X*, know *Y*, and understand *Z*" won't be sufficient. In fact, the instructional designer will push back (*should* push back) if you say this. To do her job, she will need a clear, observable description of what you need participants to be able to *do* after the training. And she may need to push further than you think is necessary on this point.
- **Become and remain open to alternative views.** As a manager, you are used to making decisions, setting direction,

and—probably—having people support your ideas and implement them. When you engage an instructional designer, you are bringing in an individual with a specialized set of knowledge and skills—knowledge and skills that should frame the form of your ultimate solution. To obtain the greatest possible outcome from a training solution, you want to take advantage of her expertise and allow it to inform and guide the process. She may even ask you to redefine your expectations of what a learning event is and isn't capable of achieving.

- **Support the instructional designer.** Open doors for her, connect her with the right people (not just those with time available), remove obstacles for her, be available to answer questions, and so on. More important, allow her the time she needs to design and develop a quality course. While there never seems to be enough time to do it right the first time, there always seems to be enough time to fix it. What you *should* fix is that way of thinking—you are the one in the position to do so. Spend the time wisely by giving the designer a chance to get it right the first time.
- **Be a champion**—Carry out the actions asked of you by the instructional designer. These may include participating in videotaped interviews to be used in the training, coordinating strategically planned enrollments (vs. open enrollment), meeting with employees before and after they attend an event to set and support expectations, distributing emails to training participants, managing employees' workloads while in training, and more.

The SME's Role

In the context of this book, you may be a SME stepping into the role of instructional designer or trainer. Or, you may be in a traditional SME role, supporting the instructional designer. If you are a SME-turned-instructional designer, this entire book is geared to you. If you are a SME-turned-trainer, this section and the next speak to your current role, and there are many strategies in Chapters 5, 6, and 7 for you to apply or support. If you are the classic SME on a project, supporting the instructional designer, here are some recommendations to guide your contributions:

- **Trust the process.** Just as you are involved in the project because of your expertise in the subject matter of the course, the instructional designer is involved because of her expertise in adult learning and course design. For the training to have the best possible outcome, you and she need to capitalize on leveraging the expertise you *both* bring. Her function is to develop the process of the course and manage which content is included and how. Your primary function is to provide, explain, and clarify content for her.
- **Confirm content accuracy.** The instructional designer will also rely on you to proofread course materials, confirm content accuracy, and correct errors in the content as needed.
- **Remain open-minded.** There are likely to be times that you and the instructional designer see things differently. You may hold views such as "we can just give *X* to the learners—it is all right here," or "I can tell them this faster than the activity she is describing," or "it will be easier to just use this—we already have it." And while you will be correct in those views, the problem arises when we recognize "giving it," "saying it," and "distributing what we already have" are not the same as learning it. (If you jumped here from the Introduction of the book, Chapter 8's Part One overview of adult learning will shed some light here, as will earlier chapters.) So, stay open to the instructional designer's expertise.
- **Commit time to your schedule.** The instructional designer will be relying on you. She will need critical inputs from you, and without them her progress will be halted. When you commit to perform an action, provide a resource, or attend a meeting, do it with the awareness that the instructional designer is relying on you to enable her to maintain the project schedule. Then block off the required time to follow through.

The Trainer's Role

Trainers are the lynchpin between course design and learning experience. With exceptional facilitation skills, you can create a meaningful and memorable learning experience even when provided with a mediocre design. Equally true though, trainer missteps can make a mess of a well-designed course. Be the former! But this section is not on facilitation strategies. Many resources exist that define the traits, characteristics, and behaviors of exceptional trainers. If you are looking for that, a succinct starting point may be ATD's Competency Model (ATD 2014). Instead, this section focuses on strategies to support you in navigating "same training in half the time" requests.

The ideas listed here complement the delivery strategies shared in Part One of this chapter. Be sure to apply both sets (Parts One and Two).

- **Recognize the business goal.** The instructional designer went to great lengths to identify the business goal and build a course supporting it. Hopefully, he also provided it to you in the overview to your facilitator guide. Without it, you are like a tour guide at the Louvre who doesn't know which wing of the largest museum in the world your group signed up to see—you can introduce them to many interesting exhibits, provide a great deal of insight on them, and still leave the guests missing what they came for. If the designer has not explicitly called out the business goal for you—ask. Depending on a number of factors, you might ask:
  - The instructional designer—if the program was designed in-house and you have access to him.
  - The project sponsor—if the program is part of an organizational, section, or department initiative and has a key figure spearheading the effort. The sponsor may be a business unit leader, an HR manager, or even a master trainer preparing you to participate in the organizational rollout. (See Chapter 1 for guidance on your conversation to define what success looks like.)
  - The manager(s) of the current cohort—if your delivery is isolated in scope to one or a few groups from the organization. (Again, the guidance in Chapter 1 for defining what success looks like will be a useful resource.)

  If you are not able to identify the business goal from the sources listed above, ask your participants what will make their investment of time in the course a success. In fact, you should ask them this even when you previously identified the desired business outcome from another source—there may be a need to align the two perspectives during the learning event.

- **Identify the connection between the business goal and the course design.** With your awareness of the ultimate goal of the training, assess the program's learning objectives and course design to see how the course materials support attaining the business goal. If you do not see the connection—ask. If you are uncertain that there *is* someone who can shed light, consider asking an L&D peer to offer his or her objective perspective on the alignment. This will help to inform decisions you may need to make in the moment during a delivery (see the trainer hacks section below for more on this).
- **Remain in the boundaries of facilitative license.** An implicit trust lies between the instructional designer and the trainer—that the designer will provide a sound design and the resources to facilitate it, and that the trainer will honor the design as she brings her personality and delivery style to the learning event. This trust should not be violated. But what if you, the trainer, receive a poorly executed design? Then what? This is where facilitative license comes in. Facilitative license is about staying true to the intent of the design while making a modification to the process (see Chapter 6 for examples of what this may look like). It is not about tossing the design and going rogue. It is not about introducing your own content or models. It is not about replacing techniques introduced in the course with your "better" techniques to achieve a given task.
- **Push beyond the end of your time with participants.** Success is not attained by you scoring all 5's on a post-course Level 1 survey. Success occurs when the new skills and knowledge introduced in training are used on the job by employees and their performance improves. You have a critical role in that process. In fact, what you do during the course is the second most influential factor in participants transferring the learning to the workplace (see Chapter 6). So, go beyond the core delivery competencies and do your part to transfer the learning. Here are a few ideas to implement:
  - Invite learners—early in the session—to determine their action planning strategies. Some may create a running list

or email themselves reminders, while others will schedule action items into their planners or be surprised that they are expected to do anything after the session. So, be prepared with suggested action planning strategies as well as resources (paper and pens) to support them.

- Connect content, activities, and practice exercises to the participants' work situations during debriefs and allow them time to work on their action plans following the debrief discussions instead of only at the end of the course.
- Close sections of the learning events as well as the overall training session with calls to action. (See Chapter 6 for more on calls to action.)

Trainer Hacks for Condensed Timing Without a Course Redesign

There may be times as a trainer that you are provided with a complete design but only afforded some fraction of that time to cover the material. If you are asked to make the modifications by redesigning the course, start in Chapter 1 and embrace the role of instructional designer. If, however, you are handed the materials and just directed to "make it work," here are a dozen time and management hacks to get you through:

Any resource you have read on training room management practices will tell you to start and end on time. We need to go beyond that sage advice when training time is constrained. We also need to address the inherent challenges you may face in adhering to the practice. So, here are your time and content management hacks—beginning with the sage advice (that is, advice from the trenches):

- **Start the session exactly on time—regardless of who has and hasn't arrived.** It may feel counterintuitive to begin when the most senior individuals have not arrived or when only a handful of people have arrived and you were expecting a room full. But what if you wait for them and they never arrive? What signal will you send to those who did arrive about the value of their time, or about when they should plan to return from breaks and lunch, or on the next day of training? When time is constrained, you may also be tempted to justify not starting on time so that "everyone begins together" thus saving overall time. Don't be lulled into that false temptation.

- **Know exactly what you will say in your opening 30 seconds**—and ensure that whatever it is will *engage them* in a meaningful way and result in learners talking for the next 7–12 minutes. This achieves three things for you: 1) you immediately begin the process of guiding learners to find their internal motivators; 2) you generate their awareness that they will be active participants in this event—not passive listeners; and 3) it takes some of the attention off of you at a time when latecomers may be walking in, allowing you to acknowledge them with a smile and gesture to an open seat for them to take quietly.
- **Provide hourly 7-minute breaks and announce the time when you will resume the session.** Most people know what 10 minutes "feels like," but I'll tell you what it feels like—15 minutes! When you set an unexpected break duration, participants note the time and return on time. When you provide consistent and predictable break times (hourly), learners can anticipate them and work within them. This last point is critical because when learners float in and out of a learning event, activity instructions need to be repeated, partnering is delayed, and a clear signal is sent to other participants that learning is not their priority—you want to avoid that.
- **Resume sessions at the time you specified—regardless of who has and hasn't returned from break.** If you miss this, the next break will run long. When you follow this guideline, you respect the time of those that who respected the boundary and place accountability in learners' hands.
- **Be prepared (after breaks) with a few minutes of valuable content when too many people are missing to jump into the vital content (see Chapter 4 for the distinction).** This way you honor the set timeline and also avoid choosing between repeating what late-returners did not hear or letting them miss it altogether.
- **Know your closing 7–12 minutes.** Providing closure to the event and a transition to how on-the-job application will occur

is as critical as your actions for generating immediate engagement at the opening were. If time is getting away from you, you must know where your alternative exits are—and they may be behind you. Instead of running through material until the clock determines your stopping point, find another exit path. When you know you will run out of time, consider choosing a theme already addressed that resonated deeply with your group, resurface it, and then connect your planned closing to it.

Time management will be critical, but it will only get you so far. When tasked with delivering an *X*-hour course in (*X*–*Y*) hours, you will need to make decisions. Here are content management ideas to guide those choices:

- **Do not cut out relationship-building elements.** For adults to actively participate and be vulnerable to the learning process, they will need to feel comfortable with you, the other participants, the environment, and the process. Instead of cutting these activities, convert them to introductions with intent (see Chapter 6) that integrate content into introductions as the group works to establish a safe learning environment.
- **Proactively identify materials to be referred to as reference material, job aids, and opportunities for further independent exploration.** Instead of saying "we are going to skip this. . . .", choose content to leave as reference that can stand alone, benefits the least from additional explanation or modeling, and so on. (See Chapter 4's valuable versus vital distinction and the process to identify vital content. You will need to answer the chapter's two questions for yourself.)
- **Be succinct and precise in your pre-activity explanations, demonstrations, and examples.** Move participants into exploratory activities and practice exercises as quickly as won't be considered reckless. Allow them to learn by doing and then clarify their questions, experiences, and your observations of their work with a rich debrief and feedback discussion.
- **Recognize that practice is critical—as is identifying the point of diminishing returns.** If one practice scenario is good,

question whether three scenarios will deliver triple the benefit. For a course design that has five application scenarios, would three be sufficient? Or, can each scenario be assigned to unique groups to complete and then chart their work for all to review? Or instead of working on reality-based but fictitious scenarios, can learners be directed to apply a skill, model, process, and so on to a challenge, project, or real-world situation of their own? All these options can save time, resulting in fewer content-editing decisions for you.

- **Convert lecture-based content to engagement opportunities.** Simply said, stop talking at people, and employ techniques that lead them to learn. Chapter 6 is all about this and includes many "instead of this, try this" examples.
- **Create out-of-seat learning opportunities.** Aside from being deeply appreciated by most chair-bound learners, aside from engaging additional learner senses resulting in increased retention, and aside from generating far greater collaboration, discussion, and idea sharing, this technique also supports your approach to hourly 7-minute breaks. A key factor in learners' dillydallying at breaks connects to their needing time out of their seats—so give it to them *as* they learn!

Final Thoughts

Adults learners have specific characteristics. They are internally motivated and want to be self-directed; they bring life experiences and knowledge to learning events; they are goal-oriented, relevancy-oriented, and practical; and they like to be respected. To be successful, your course design and facilitation choices need to respect these traits. Have you heard the saying "when a hammer is your only tool, every problem looks like a nail"? Well, you now have many tools in addition to your hammer. Use them to build courses that address the root causes of workplace performance issues and that provide adult learners with the environment and factors they need to succeed.

Put It Into Practice

Early in the chapter you were asked to reread the six characteristics of adult learners noted by Malcolm Knowles. Your ability to recite them so you can honor them in your designs was called out as critical. Test yourself. Write them down—or what you recall of them. They are reprinted at the end of this chapter so you can check your work—so don't accidentally look ahead!

Adult Learner Characteristics

1.

2.

3.

4.

5.

6.

Chapter Actions

- ❑ Create a job aid to display at your desk that identifies Knowles' six characteristics of adult learners. Make it visual, colorful, and eye-catching. Then refer to it frequently.
- ❑ Determine if each training request is really what your organization requires to succeed. If it isn't, prepare to argue against wasting time, money, and effort on training that will not support the organization's goals.
- ❑ Refer to Chapters 5, 6, and 7 of this book and the ADDIE model in this chapter as you build course designs.
- ❑ Review the trainer strategies in this chapter each time you prepare to deliver a course.
- ❑ Revisit your chapter-by-chapter action plan in Chapter 10 and update it with actions related to the content of this chapter.

Check Your Work

Here are the six characteristics of adult learners noted by Malcolm Knowles (1984):

- Adults need to know why learning something is important before they learn it.
- Adults have a concept of self and do not like others imposing their will on them.
- Adults have a wealth of knowledge and experience and want that knowledge to be recognized.
- Adults open up to learning when they think that the learning will help them with real problems.
- Adults want to know how the learning will help them immediately.
- Adults learn in response to internal (versus external) motivations.

9

Where Do I Go From Here?

Better Training, Half the Time

You really can have *better* training in half the time. If you follow the strategies and ideas in this book—with fearless authenticity and grit—you will find that better training in any time frame is within your grasp:

- You can develop shorter trainings that deliver meaningful results.
- You can condense existing programs into shorter events that the business values.
- You can satisfy learners' desire for effective, on-demand learning experiences that respect their time and attention spans.
- You can achieve better results with shorter events than you currently do with longer programs.
- And—the best of all—instead of continuing to fulfill potentially misguided training requests at a breakneck pace, you can shift from reacting to training requests you receive to driving what training looks like in your organization!

When you implement the simple but powerful strategies found throughout these chapters, you will begin to build a reputation for creating highly sought-after, engaging programs. You will gain confidence in your skills and ability to build programs that actually help employees perform better. You will be known for learning events that are practical, mission-critical, and value-added. And you will be able to do so with less stress and more peace in the process.

Return to the activities that you walked through in the chapters as often as you need to. Choose Chapter Actions that fit with your role and your projects and add them to your calendar. Use the tools in Chapter 10 to bring clarity and energy to your work. Share them with partners and colleagues who are also striving to create and deliver meaningful learning events in less time and with less stress.

I know that you are a busy professional and that you won't be able to implement every idea in this book. That's OK. I am equally certain that you will be able to use many of them as real lifelines in a time crunch. And you will be able to create space in your work to catch your breath, take stock, and move ahead with strategies that really work—no matter your role in talent development.

Here is your call to action: Throughout the chapters, you have been encouraged to create your own action plan. Take a moment now to consider it (whether you used Chapter 10's chapter-by-chapter action plan, the Put It Into Practice and Chapter Actions sections throughout, or another system) and choose your top three priorities to start working on. One of the priorities you choose should be something you can do immediately—that is intended as more of an encouragement than a requirement! Remember the theme that has run throughout this whole book . . . until you *do* something with what you have learned, learning hasn't transferred.

Best of luck to you. My passion is to share what I have learned along the way to make the journey more fun and less challenging for those who follow the same path as well as to continue my own growth. I would enjoy hearing your thoughts and comments about training and the ideas presented in this book. Visit my blog at KimberlyDevlin.com.

10

The Tools for Better Training in Half the Time

Worksheets, Assessments, and Job Aids

The tools presented here were created to help you deliver better training in half the time. Some are intended to support you as you work through the book, and others are to guide and assist you in implementing strategies from the book. To go a level deeper with them, compare them to the tools you are designing, developing, and distributing to learners to aid their development continuum. How do these resources help you extend the takeaways from the chapters, and how can you build resources that do the same thing for your learners?

You can download pdf versions of the tools from KimberlyDevlin.com and reproduce them for use in your work and projects. Please always reproduce them with the copyright credit line clearly visible.

Tools Included in *Same Training, Half the Time*

Introduction

✓ Assessment: Jumpstart *Better* Training in Half the Time
✓ Worksheet: Chapter-by-Chapter Summary Sheet and Action Plan

Chapter 1

- ✓ Assessment: Using the Five A's to Move the Finish Line
- ✓ Worksheet: Using the Five A's to Move the Finish Line
- ✓ Job Aid: Language Aligned With the Five A's for Moving the Finish Line

Chapter 2

- ✓ Worksheet: Earning Your Seat at the Table

Chapter 4

- ✓ Job Aid: Getting to the Essential Content

Chapter 5

- ✓ Assessment: How Well Are You Reclaiming Pre-Training Time?
- ✓ Job Aid: Sample Instruments Managers Can Use to Set Learning Plans With Employees
- ✓ Worksheet: Pre-Course Trainer Email Worksheet
- ✓ Job Aid: Sample Email from Trainer

Chapter 6

- ✓ Assessment: How Well Are You Maximizing Your Limited Training Time?

Chapter 7

- ✓ Assessment: How Well Are You Reclaiming Post-Training Time?
- ✓ Sample Instrument: Post-Training Checkpoint Meeting—Learner Version
- ✓ Sample Instrument: Post-Training Checkpoint Meeting—Manager Version

Introduction Assessment: Jumpstart *Better* Training in Half the Time

Currently, in an effort to meet the goal of creating and delivering training in a time crunch you and your training team may be scrambling and using coping strategies such as these and more:

- Shifting the burden to learners with a "pre-work dump."
- Cutting out application activities (you know, the engaging, effective parts of training).
- Forgoing adequate scaffolding for and debriefing of exercises.
- Ending sessions with "we can cover the rest next time."
- Spending nights and weekends attempting to create inappropriate deliverables to meet unrealistic deadlines for programs that don't add value.

Whatever your coping strategies, there is hope. The ideas presented in this book can help you catch your breath and learn how to create better training in less time. Start the journey by answering these three questions:

1. What are you looking to get out of this book?

2. How would you define your current challenge related to same training in half the time?

3. What will be your implementation strategy for action planning as you discover and explore the ideas, strategies, and techniques presented in this book? *(Use the worksheet that follows to help you build an action plan. Keep it close at hand as you work through the chapters.)*

Introduction Worksheet: Chapter-by-Chapter Summary Sheet and Action Plan

	Overview	My Takeaways	What I Will Do As A Result
Introduction	The challenges driving increased demands on learning, the conundrum of "same training in half the time" requests, and the promise that you can have *better* training in half the time.		1. 2. 3.
Chapter 1	Using the Five A's to move the finish line on your projects (Appreciate, Acknowledge, Ask, Apprehension, and Alternatives).		1. 2. 3.
Chapter 2	Earning a seat at the decision-making table, and doing it in a way that your voice is listened to.		1. 2. 3.
Chapter 3	Strategies to make learners' needs your first priority without alienating your project sponsors.		1. 2. 3.
Chapter 4	Identify essential content using two powerful questions—what does success look like, and does this content bring us closer to that goal?		1. 2. 3.

Chapter 5	Pre-training strategies to reclaim development time and enhance the effectiveness of learning events.		1. 2. 3.
Chapter 6	Training strategies to enhance the effectiveness of learning events.		1. 2. 3.
Chapter 7	Post-training strategies to reclaim development time and enhance the effectiveness of transfer of learning to the workplace.		1. 2. 3.
Chapter 8	A primer in the theory that drives effective learning and strategies for those in sideline roles that support the instructional designer.		1. 2. 3.
Chapter 9	A reminder that better training in half the time can be your reality—when you hold true to the tenets of sound instructional design, and an invitation to stay connected.		1. 2. 3.
Chapter 10	Worksheets, assessments, and job aids to help you apply the ideas in this book—and to set a model for you to emulate in your course designs.		1. 2. 3.

Chapter 1 Assessment: Using the Five A's to Move the Finish Line

Consider each step of the model in the first column and the associated action(s) in the second column. Then give an honest assessment of how well you are doing these things today—not how well you *have* done or *could* do them but *are* doing them. Next, complete the grid on the next page.

Step in the Model	**Description of the Step**	Doing exceptionally	Doing well	Doing poorly	Not on my radar
1–Appreciate	Convey genuine thanks for being brought in and enhance your understanding (appreciation) of the request	❐	❐	❐	❐
2–Acknowledge	Recognize the criticality of the request	❐	❐	❐	❐
3–Ask	Clarify details of the request	❐	❐	❐	❐
4–Apprehension	Raise key concerns in a non-confrontational manner	❐	❐	❐	❐
5–Alternatives	Present options	❐	❐	❐	❐

For items you are performing exceptionally, please visit my blog at KimberlyDevlin.com to share examples of your language, tactics, and insider tips.	How can you leverage the actions you are doing well and exceptionally?
What sample language, from Chapter 1, will improve the actions you rated as "doing poorly"?	Consider the items not on your radar, why aren't they? Do you feel they fall outside your responsibility or authority? Who can help create space for them in your role?

Chapter 1 Worksheet: Using the Five A's to Move the Finish Line

What is your plan to move the finish line? Complete the worksheet below by referring to the job aid on the following pages, considering your communication style, and factoring in your unique knowledge of the project sponsor and his request.

Moving the Finish Line

	My Planned Language	Possible Responses	My Redirect/ Probing Questions
#1 Appreciate			
#2 Acknowledge			
#3 Ask			
#4 Apprehension			
#5 Alternatives			

Check Yourself:

Before practicing the conversation, consider these self-reflection questions and revise your plan as needed.

1. During Appreciate, sincerity is essential. Will you mean what you say if you say what you wrote?

2. Appreciate and Acknowledge are relationship builders. Are you demonstrating respect with your planned phrases? How might you revise them to enhance their relationship-building value?

3. Do your Alternatives achieve these three goals?
   - ❑ Maintain elements of the original request
   - ❑ Draw parallels to your prior successes
   - ❑ Clearly state how they will benefit the requestor

Chapter 1 Job Aid:
Language Aligned With the Five A's for Moving the Finish Line

As you plan your approach to moving the finish line, consider the following sample language to use during the sequential Appreciate, Acknowledge, Ask, Apprehension, and Alternatives steps.

1—Appreciate

To show your appreciation for being asked to help, try:

- "Thank you for letting me talk through this with you."
- "I appreciate your thinking about performance support in relation to this initiative."
- "It is always a pleasure to explore needs with your team."
- "Thank you for thinking of me to look at this with you."
- "I am grateful for the advance notice on this project request—this doesn't always happen."
- "Thank you for your call."

To develop an appreciation for the request as made, use broad questions such as these:

- "What can you tell me about why you want to do this now?"
- "What or who is the driving force behind this request?"
- "How did you arrive at this proposed course of action?"
- "Were there alternative approaches you considered or tried?"

2—Acknowledge

Acknowledge is about being supportive of the request (and the requestor) while maintaining neutrality on the ultimate direction the request will take. Try:

- "I understand how critical this is."
- "I can see where you are coming from."
- "Certainly, it makes sense that the staff/team/group will need support in the transition."
- "Yes, I agree that time is precious and recognize the operational constraints your team works within."

- "I can see you have given this a great deal of thought."
- "I do see the path of events that brought you to this point."
- "Yes, I can certainly appreciate the position you are in."
- "This all makes sense as you have laid it out."

3—Ask

Remembering to break down the stated desired outcome into its individual building blocks, the key question stem here is:

- "Am I hearing you correctly that. . . . ?"

4—Apprehension

Begin with your greatest concern:

- "Here is my one concern. . . ."
- "We certainly could do that. I'm just thinking about _________ and contemplating how we can best avoid ___________."
- "We could certainly do that. I'm just worried that you're not going to get the results you're looking for."

5—Alternatives

Consider moving into Alternatives using "starter language" such as:

- "When you suggested that we _______________ it sparked an idea for me. . . ."
- "I certainly hear where you're coming from. Are you open to hearing how I see this and some slightly different approaches?"
- "Initially, this may sound radically different than what you're asking for, but it has the same foundational elements, and I believe it will be a great way to get to your goal."
- "I get the feeling that you are receptive to additional ideas. What would you think of . . . ?"
- "I'd like to run a few ideas past you to see what your thoughts are on them."

As you present your alternatives, the following language can be used to connect your ideas to their ideas and to the goal they want to achieve:

- "You suggested that we __________, and I agree that we should do that [or some specific part of it you agree with]. I would only add that we should also __________."
- "What would you say if I suggested that we think about _____."
- "Based on my experience on previous projects, I'm confident we'll have greater success in reaching your goal if we consider. . . ."
- "Based on prior projects' experiences, I'd like to suggest a few alternatives for your consideration."
- "Based on prior projects, I recommend __________."
- "I'm thinking out loud here, but here is what is coming to mind for me—and I'd really like your input on this. . . ."
- "So, what if we. . . ."
- "What if, instead of *X*, we were to _______________?"
- "Do you know what I think would really get you where you're looking to be on this project? I suggest we should think about __________."

If you meet resistance, the following phrases can allow you to remain persistent without being perceived as pushy:

- "Ultimately, the final decision will be yours; I would just like to strongly suggest you consider. . . ."
- "I would like to suggest we stay open to the idea of _________."
- "If you are still open to alternative ideas—which I think will get you greater results—I'm happy to put together some thoughts to show to you."
- "I really want this project to be a success for you. Would it be okay for me to mock up some examples of what I am envisioning for your review? We can walk through the examples together and see what will work best."

Chapter 2 Worksheet: Earning Your Seat at the Table

First, determine which statements apply to your current situation that having a seat at the table could correct. Check all that apply and add any relevant dynamics not listed. My clients . . .

- ❑ Bring me in late in the game when projects have training needs associated with them.
- ❑ Expect training to be developed and deployed in unrealistic timeframes.
- ❑ Look to the training team to develop training in isolation (without meaningful input and contributions from the subject matter resources).
- ❑ Frequently provide a slide deck, tell me they have done most of the work, and ask me to "turn it into training."
- ❑ Expect training to "fix" performance problems.
- ❑ Want to eliminate line items for customizing programs from proposals.
- ❑ Routinely say the training program doesn't need much—just some "prettying up."
- ❑
- ❑
- ❑

Next, review design projects you completed in the past 18 months. For each, identify what you accomplished. Think *business results*, not deliverables!

Project	Business Results Achieved

Finally, identify who your champions are and list them here.

Chapter 4 Job Aid: Getting to the Essential Content

Question One: What Does Success Look Like?

Consider these variations on "what does success look like?":

- "What would you like to see happening after this training that isn't happening now?"
- "What should participants be able to do as a result of completing the training?"
- "If I observed an employee performing to your expectations after the training, what would I see?"
- "So that we can measure the effectiveness of the solution we develop, in one sentence, what would you say is the goal of this training?"
- "Of all the skills the participants should possess, which are most critical to his or her success?"
- "What are the two things personnel are doing or not doing today that create the greatest number of undesired situations for you or the organization?"
- "What metrics will the employees be held accountable for achieving?"
- "What are the criteria the participants will be evaluated against in their performance evaluations?"

Here are some sample follow-up questions—to probe, to clarify, and to add specificity. (Note: your follow-up questions will depend on the answers that are provided to the initial questions asked.)

- "OK, *X*-ing by using which skills exactly?"
- "Thank you for that. And what differentiates an effective *X* [clerk, supervisor, machinist] from an ineffective one?"
- "Will you tell me three specific things the employee would need to do to rise to that statement?"
- "And what is the one behavior that is most critical to them meeting that goal? And the second most critical behavior?"

Question Two: Does this get us closer to success?

Consider these variations on the second question:

- "Does this bring us closer to success? How?"
- "Can you tell me how this supports your goal?"
- "What, specifically, will the participants be required to do with this knowledge when performing their jobs?"
- "What is the direct line connection between this content and employees' performance requirements?"

Chapter 5 Assessment: How Well Are You Reclaiming Pre-Training Time?

Consider each action in the first column and give an honest assessment of how well you are doing these things today—not how well you *have* done or *could* do them but *are* doing them.

I am currently . . .	Exceptionally well	Room for Improvement	Not at all	My Plan to Enhance My Use of This Strategy
Creating tiny training to engage learners in the learning event before they arrive.	❐	❐	❐	
Providing learners with access to optional pre-course content and exercises (this is not pre-reading).	❐	❐	❐	
Educating managers on their pre-training role.	❐	❐	❐	
Developing tools that inform managers of course content and skills so they can establish learning expectations with staff.	❐	❐	❐	
Creating tools managers can use in pre-training meetings with employees.	❐	❐	❐	

I am currently . . .	Exceptionally well	Room for Improvement	Not at all	My Plan to Enhance My Use of This Strategy
Drafting messages for the facilitator to send to participants before training.	❒	❒	❒	
Drafting communications for managers to share with employees prior to training.	❒	❒	❒	
Preparing learners with what is required to fully participate in the learning event.	❒	❒	❒	
Exciting learners about the training prior to arriving.	❒	❒	❒	
Setting expectations for learners' participation in advance of the session.	❒	❒	❒	
Leveraging pre-work to engage learners (versus dumping volumes of reading on them).	❒	❒	❒	
Saving class time by providing self-paced assessments to complete before arriving.	❒	❒	❒	

Chapter 5 Job Aid: Sample Instruments Managers Can Use to Set Learning Plans With Employees

Setting Learning Plans—Option 1

This sample planning tool is based on the Johari Window's four quadrants (originally used as a model for mapping personality awareness). It is one of a few options included here that you can model an instrument off of.

	Known to Self	Unknown to Self
Known to Others	*Manager and employee collaborate in this region to identify learning goals based on the employee's strengths and weaknesses known to both of them.*	*Manager records learning goal items here based on employee's strengths and weaknesses known only to the manager.*
Unknown to Others	*Employee records learning goal items here based on strengths and weaknesses known only to the employee.*	*This space will be left blank prior to training. During the course, the employee adds to this quadrant as these double-blind areas are identified.*

Chapter 5 Job Aid, continued

Setting Learning Plans—Option 2

This sample planning tool can be used to straddle the learning event. The top half would be completed prior to training, and the bottom half would be completed during training. After training, the employee and manager can meet to compare the plan to the course experience and to decide on the employee's implementation approach.

Contributions You Will Make Record your strengths in relation to this training, and how you will leverage them to contribute during the learning event.	**Your Learning Goals** Based on the course description, learning objectives, and your current development needs, record three specific learning goals you will achieve in this class: 1. 2. 3.
Validate Your Instincts Use this space during the learning event to record validations you receive on your current practices (what you are doing well).	**New Discoveries** Use this space during the learning event to record what you are learning that will inform your actions going forward.

Chapter 5 Job Aid, continued

Setting Learning Plans—Option 3

If this sample tool is selected, you may encourage the manager and employee to create a participation plan in proportion to the sizes of the pieces of the graphic.

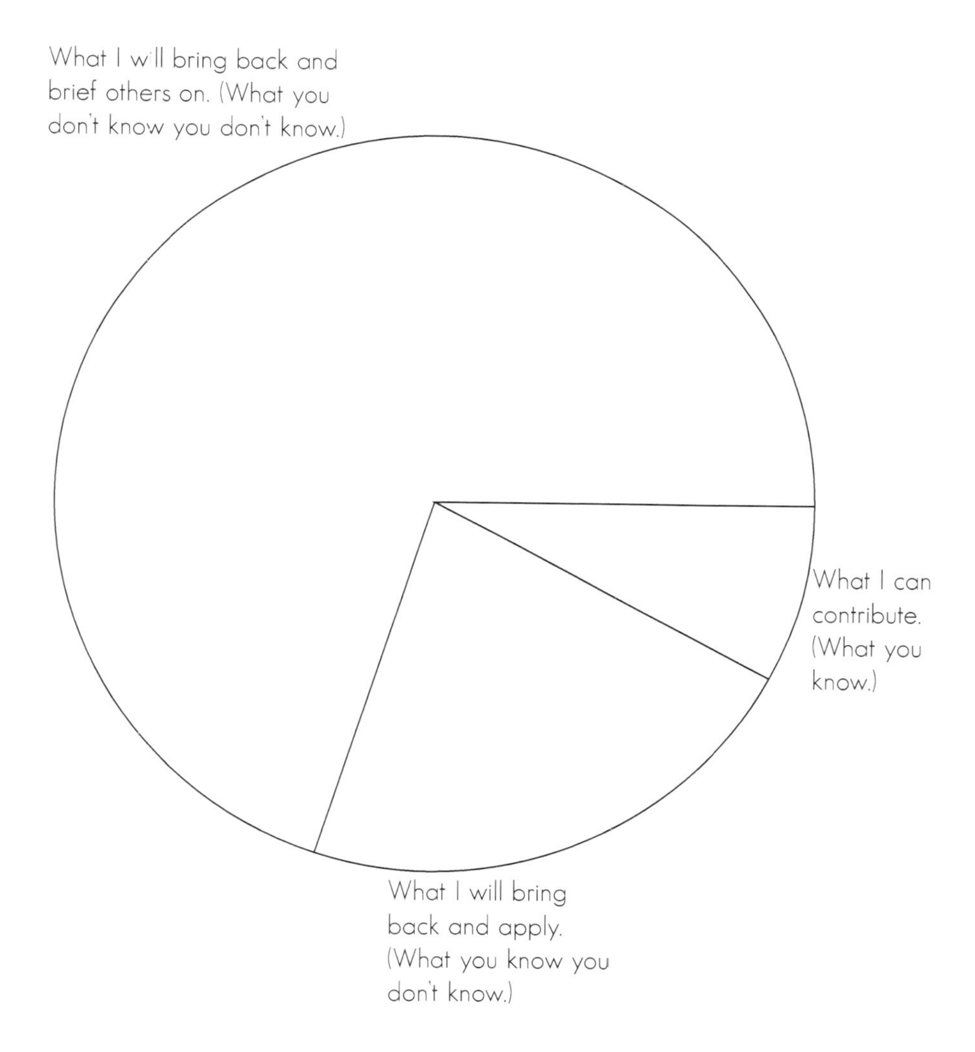

Chapter 5 Worksheet: Pre-Course Trainer Email Worksheet

Use this worksheet to guide you in drafting a pre-training message to be sent to learners from the trainer.

Elements	Tips for Success	My Drafted Language
Greeting	✓ Highlight that this copy will need to be edited to match the time of day the email is sent.	
Generate enthusiasm	✓ State benefits of course. ✓ Share personal experience with course content (be specific).	
Set expectations	✓ Highlight interactive nature of course. ✓ List required elements (pre-work, what to bring, assignments, and so on). ✓ Introduce any out-of-class requirements.	
Share pre-work	✓ Infuse a sense of enthusiasm. ✓ Indicate estimated time to complete.	
Share learning goals	✓ Bullet point the learning objectives—streamline them if needed for ease of comprehension and to enhance first impressions.	
Request confirmation of receipt	✓ Ensure the message was received and begin establishing a course culture of accountability.	
Close	✓ Include a signature line with contact information.	

Chapter 5 Job Aid: Sample Email From Trainer

SUBJECT LINE: Pre-Work Required for the Contracting for Construction Services Series

Good morning/afternoon [tailor] -

Are you as excited as I am for you? The Contracting for Construction Services training series ("*Getting to the Certificate of Occupancy*") will begin in a few weeks and presents a tremendous professional growth opportunity for you. As a preview to the learning, I have included the overall goals for the series at the bottom of this email.

This multi-session series will be highly interactive, requiring your active participation during each session and a small amount of preparation and activity between sessions and prior to the program. To ensure the best use of face-to-face time for discussions and debates, these assignments are required to be completed prior to attending each session.

See just how easy (and interesting!) these assignments will be by completing the initial pre-work now. Plan on spending 10-12 minutes on it.

Pre-Work:

1. Read the brief article, *What Really Sank the Titanic* at [link]
2. Arrive prepared to discuss the relevance of the Titanic article to contracting for construction services. Use the following questions to guide your comments:
    - What factors appear to have contributed to the sinking of the Titanic?
    - How often have the same factors affected an agency project?
    - Who was/is responsible for those decisions? On the Titanic? On an agency project?
    - When do *you* take action to avoid future problems? (Be specific!)
    - What can be done to avoid such an outcome? (Be specific!)

Series Goals:
Through your active participation in activities and assignments, you can expect to develop the skills to:

1. Recognize agency resources and their roles in the construction procurement process.
2. Put out a construction solicitation using the best-suited method and instrument.
3. Follow state statutes and agency preferences that apply to construction procurements.
4. Participate in multiple types of contractor selection processes.
5. Manage a construction project in accordance with its specifications.
6. Detect fraud, abuse, or collusion.
7. Close out a construction project in adherence with established best practices.

Your **confirmation of receipt** that this arrived will be appreciated.

Thank you ~

Chapter 6 Assessment: How Well Are You Maximizing Your Limited Training Time?

Consider each action in the first column and give an honest assessment of how well you are doing these things today—not how well you *have* done or *could* do them but *are* doing them.

I am currently. . . .	Exceptionally well	Room for Improvement	Not at all	My Plan to Enhance My Use of This Strategy
Designing activities that engage learners.	❐	❐	❐	
Designing activities that allow for personal reflection.	❐	❐	❐	
Designing activities that cause learners to work–hard.	❐	❐	❐	
Designing activities that let learners play–with purpose.	❐	❐	❐	
Designing activities that let learners fail in a safe setting.	❐	❐	❐	
Designing activities that set learners up for success.	❐	❐	❐	
Creating course designs that mine for content instead of pushing content onto learners.	❐	❐	❐	
Honoring adult learners' experience and existing knowledge through design choices.	❐	❐	❐	
Challenging learners.	❐	❐	❐	
Creating exploratory learning activities that lead participants to pre-defined outcomes.	❐	❐	❐	

I am currently. . . .	Exceptionally well	Room for Improvement	Not at all	My Plan to Enhance My Use of This Strategy
Curating learning events to provide vital and targeted learning experiences.	❒	❒	❒	
Creating meaningful context for learners.	❒	❒	❒	
Designing introductions with intent that integrate content in participant introductions.	❒	❒	❒	
Building time into courses for individual goal setting.	❒	❒	❒	
Ensuring course activities require learners to apply content instead of merely recall it.	❒	❒	❒	
Protecting time for both independent and guided self-reflection during the course.	❒	❒	❒	
Integrating calls to action in my courses through action planning, application assignments, and other techniques.	❒	❒	❒	
Engaging multiple learner senses in learning activities.	❒	❒	❒	
Providing trainer support by giving them options to work within.	❒	❒	❒	
Providing trainer support by creating facilitator guides with effective layout and content choices.	❒	❒	❒	
Providing trainer support by making trainer resources easy to locate and navigate.	❒	❒	❒	

Chapter 7 Assessment: How Well Are You Reclaiming Post-Training Time?

Consider each action in the first column and give an honest assessment of how well you are doing these things today—not how well you *have* done or *could* do them but *are* doing them.

I am currently. . .	Exceptionally Well	Room for Improvement	Not at all	My Plan to Enhance My Use of This Strategy
Drafting messages for the facilitator to send to participants after training.	❐	❐	❐	
Drafting communications for managers to share with employees after training.	❐	❐	❐	
Creating social media discussion areas for learners to collaborate with one another after training.	❐	❐	❐	
Building job-embedded application assignments into course designs.	❐	❐	❐	
Developing learning boosters to provide periodic infusions of renewed focus on the learning in the days, weeks, and months after training.	❐	❐	❐	
Prompting managers to maintain a post-training focus on course content and its implementation.	❐	❐	❐	

I am currently. . . .	Exceptionally Well	Room for Improvement	Not at all	My Plan to Enhance My Use of This Strategy
Creating tools managers can use after training to reinforce and acknowledge employees' implementation efforts.	❐	❐	❐	
Keeping managers informed of post-training resources and boosters being made available to employees.	❐	❐	❐	
Educating managers on their post-training role.	❐	❐	❐	
Building evaluation into project plans to support transfer of learning.	❐	❐	❐	

Chapter 7 Sample Instrument
Post-Training Checkpoint Meeting—Learner Version

Purpose of Discussion:

1. Inform your direct supervisor of how the learning benefited you.
2. Share your plan to implement your new skills and knowledge.
3. Request support you will need to successfully integrate the new behaviors.

Length of Meeting: 15 minutes

Prepare for the Discussion: Use this worksheet to gather your thoughts and plan what you will share.

1. *Inform your direct supervisor of how the learning benefited you:*
   What I hoped to learn, and did, was: ____________________
   I was surprised to learn: ____________________
   Attending the course and applying what I learned will benefit me by:____
   ____
   Applying what I learned will benefit the department/organization by: ____
   ____

2. *Share your plan to implement your new skills and knowledge:*
   The training confirmed I should CONTINUE to: ____________________
   From what I have learned, I plan to STOP doing: ____________________
   I also plan to START to:
   - ____________________
   - ____________________
   - ____________________

3. *Request support you will need to successfully integrate the new behaviors:*
   Generally, in the next [*timeframe*] (week? two weeks? month?) as I start using the course content, it would help me if you could . . .

   And, in specific support of my Continue, Stop, Start plan (above), I would appreciate your support by . . .

Chapter 7 Sample Instrument
Post-Training Checkpoint Meeting—Manager Version

Purpose of Discussion:

1. Receive a briefing from your employee on how the learning benefited him/her.
2. Learn the employee's plan to implement new skills and knowledge.
3. Extend support the employee will need to successfully integrate the new behaviors.

Length of Meeting: 15 minutes
Prepare for the Discussion: Use these questions to help prompt the employee through the discussion.

1. *Receive a briefing from your employee on how the learning benefited him/her:*
   - How will the course content help you improve your performance?
   - What did you learn that surprised you?
   - How did attending the course benefit you?
   - How will applying strategies from the course benefit you?
   - What benefit will the department/organization realize as you apply the courses' strategies, tools, and new knowledge?
2. *Learn the employee's plan to implement new skills and knowledge:*
   - What did the training validate that you are already doing well? (to continue)
   - Based on what you learned, what actions and behaviors will you stop demonstrating? (to stop)
   - Of all the ideas you left the course with, what are the top three things you intend to do differently going forward? (to start)
3. *Extend support the employee will need to successfully integrate the new behaviors:*
   - When you think about the next [timeframe] (week? two weeks? month?) and the changes you want to make, what can I do to create space for you to make those changes?
   - And, what do you specifically need from me to support you in implementing your Continue, Stop, Start plan (above)?

REFERENCES

ATD. (2014). ATD Competency Model. Alexandria, VA: Association for Talent Development (ATD), formerly ASTD. Available at https://www.td.org/certification/atd-competency-model.

Broad, M.L., and J.W. Newstrom. (1992). *Transfer of Training: Action Packed Strategies to Ensure High Payoff from Training Investment.* New York: Basic.

Kirkpatrick, D.L., and J.D Kirkpatrick. (2006). *Evaluating Training Programs: The Four Levels*, 3d ed. San Francisco: Berrett-Koehler.

Knowles, M. (1984). *The Adult Learner: A Neglected Species*, 3d ed. Houston, TX: Gulf.

McCambridge, J., J. Wilton, and D.R. Elbourne. (2013). "Systematic Review of the Hawthorne Effect: New Concepts Are Needed to Study Research Participation Effects." *Journal of Epidemiology*, March 67(3): 267-277.

ACKNOWLEDGMENTS

Were it not for the talented and generous professionals I have been so fortunate to cross paths with, this book would not have been possible. Their invaluable gifts of insight, encouragement, guidance, redirection, and development have left their mark on me and this book. Thank you Susan. Thank you Ronnie.

Crafting this book would also not have been possible without the direction, support, and patience of the TPH team. Thank you Cat and Jacki.

Lastly, to those who helped create space for me to write this book—thank you Dad, Ronnie, Mick, and Nicky. Each of you, in your own way, made this possible.

ABOUT THE AUTHOR

Kimberly Devlin is both president of Poetic License, Inc., a business communication consulting firm, and managing director of EdTrek, Inc., a training and development consulting firm. She specializes in helping client organizations realize business objectives through strategic planning, organization-wide training implementations, service standard creation, train-the-trainer certifications, and other initiatives.

With a MA in journalism and BA in English literature from the University of Miami and her Certified Professional in Learning and Performance (CPLP) credential, Kimberly leverages her communication skills and training and development qualifications to create highly effective, sought-out learning events. Among her most professionally rewarding projects are developing the skills of other industry professionals through online and face-to-face facilitations as well as authoring. Her other titles include *Facilitation Skills Training* (ATD 2017) and *Customer Service Training* (ATD 2015), both in the bestselling ATD Workshop Series.

As a writer, instructional designer, facilitator, speaker, and consultant with more than 20 years' industry experience, she has provided technical assistance nationally and internationally, has presented at international and industry-specific conferences, and has been featured in ATD's *TD* magazine for her status as a CPLP pilot pioneer.

Kimberly lives in south Florida and receives regular reminders from her dog that there is more to life than professional accomplishments alone.

ABOUT TPH

We believe that learning and training are key drivers in achieving the results you want in your life and in your business. We also believe that you shouldn't have to do that all on your own. To that end, we specialize in bringing you compelling ideas from innovative authors who have the expertise to coach you to success. We publish world-class business and talent development content from established experts in the field who share not only their experience and best practices but also the practical tools and resources you—and your organization—need to achieve excellence.

You want to be your best. We want to help.

Visit our website: www.trainerspublishinghouse.com.

Made in the USA
Lexington, KY
03 December 2018